Maternal Health Care

Study of Janani Suraksha Yojana (JSY) in Uttarakhand

Maternal Health Care

Study of Janani Suraksha Yojana (JSY) in Uttarakhand

Archana Sinha

Indian Social Institute

GYAN

First Published, 2018

Published by

Gyan Publishing House
5, Ansari Road
Daryaganj, New Delhi-110002
Phone: 9811692060
E-mail: books@gyanbooks.com

and

Indian Social Institute
10, Institutional Area
Lodi Road, New Delhi - 110003
Phone: (011) 49534132/133

Printed at: G. Print Process, Delhi.

Cataloging in Publication Data—DK
Courtesy: D.K. Agencies (P) Ltd. <docinfo@dkagencies.com>

Sinha, Archana, *Dr.*, author.
Mental health care : study of Janani Suraksha Yojana (JSY) in Uttarakhand / Archana Sinha.
pages cm
Study conducted in Almora and Haridwar districts of Uttarakhand, India.
Includes bibliographical references and index.
ISBN 9788189762674 (hardback)

1. Janani Suraksha Yojana. 2. Maternal health services—Government policy—India—Almora (District) 3. Maternal health services—Government policy—India—Haridwar (District) 4. Rural health services—India—Almora (District) 5. Rural health services—India—Haridwar (District) I. Indian Social Institute, publisher. II. Title.

LCC RG965.I42A46 2018 | DDC 362.1982095451 23

Contents

List of Tables

List of Cases

Foreword

Reduction of maternal mortality is an area of concern for the Governments across the globe. Despite various initiatives at national and global level, maternal mortality continues to be high in developing countries. Maternal health care for women who are poor, and facing multiple vulnerabilities and biases continues to be inadequate. Health budgets, adequate, skilled, gender sensitive health personnel, remain inadequate. Services don't reach the mothers who need them, even years after schemes such as Janani Suraksha Yojana (JSY) are launched. Expenditures on institutional deliveries still occur, which for poor families is significant enough to prefer home deliveries. It is just not care at childbirth that the mothers need, but the various other determinants of health that matter.

The **"Maternal Health Care: Study of Janani Suraksha Yojana (JSY) in Uttarakhand"** by Dr. Archana Sinha, taking Almora and Haridwar as sample districts is an extremely valuable contribution to the understanding of the causes behind the maternal mortality in Uttarakhand. Maternal mortality was to have been brought down to 100 by 2012 in spite of Uttarakhand being a high focus state of the National Rural Health Mission. Still a significant number of home deliveries take place because of the difficult terrain, lack of transport facilities, distances and costs involved, because the hard reality of the lives of these women, care to these mothers should also be facilitated, even as provision of comprehensive maternal care, safe childbirth and post natal care in institutions is ensured , with possibility of quick referral. Safe delivery, survival of mother and newborn needs ensuring, not just ensuring institutional delivery.

The presence of skilled birth attendants, who are adequately supported by a strengthened public health system, with skills and essential medicines needed for emergency situations like Post Partum Haemorrhage (PPH) has to be ensured. Bleeding is the commonest cause of maternal death, especially when so many of our mothers are anaemic. The continued high level of maternal deaths, even though Maternal Mortality Rate (MMR) has shown a decline is too unacceptably high in some parts and indeed a matter of shame for us as a society. This was the only Millennium Development Goal (MDG) that was not met, hope Sustainable Development Goals (SDGs) are met. The issue is not just of meeting goals, but meeting the mothers' Right to Live as Guaranteed in the Constitution Article 21.

Way back when Munshi Prem Chand wrote the gut wrenching story "Kafan" about poor man Budhia and his wife who dies painfully in labour, one did not understand then that it was about a poor mother dying, writhing in pain from obstructed labour. This was years ago. Why should mothers continue to die from bleeding, sepsis, toxemias of pregnancy, malnourishment, anaemia, etc. when it is possible to prevent their deaths and ensure survival without most of these complications?

Maternal health is a key indicator of functional health system. Maternal health must be addressed as a part of gamut of care that connects essential maternal, and newborn health services. There are however, constraints like lack of adequate government health facilities equipped and functional to provide comprehensive obstetric services for mother and newborn. The mothers and newborns need much better care and support than what they receive in many parts, especially if they are poor and the new born is a girl child. The mothers need the care not only because SDGs have to be met but because the other children in the family need them and because mothers irrespective of how poor they are have a right to live, deliver safely, with dignity ensured to them. Dr. Archana Sinha has identified the gaps in implementation through her study and with the various case studies has made valuable recommendations. This outstanding research reports provides good insight into implementation successes and problems with India's National Health Mission. This study is a valuable contribution to the understanding of this extremely important concern related to Maternal Health Care, the Janani Suraksha Yojana. Hope a follow up study after few years will be undertaken documenting the positive changes and bridging of the gaps identified as poor mothers of Uttarakhand and as in every other region they need and deserve much more.

Dr Mira Shiva M.D.

Acknowledgements

I acknowledge and express my sincere appreciation and thanks to all those persons who have been associated with the study **"Maternal Health Care: Study of Janani Suraksha Yojana (JSY) in Uttarakhand"** and have helped to bring it to completion. My sincere thanks to Dr. Denzil Fernandes (Executive Director, Indian Social Institute, New Delhi), Dr. Joe Xavier (Former Executive Director, Indian Social Institute, New Delhi) and Dr. Paul D'Souza for their continuous support and guidance to bring the study to completion.

I acknowledge support and help rendered from field based organizations and agencies in Uttarakhand, which extended their support -Aman Trust from Almora and Adarsh Yuva Samiti (AYUS) from Haridwar, for their help in coordinating the data collection work through their dedicated team members. I am thankful to all those beneficiaries' and non beneficiaries' respondents from the field for giving their precious time during filling up questionnaires in the field. Mr. Jeet Singh and Mr. Siprian Kiro deserve my thanks for their active participation and help in initiating the field investigation and data collection from the field as research staff of project team.

I further extend my thanks to the faculty and staff members at Indian Social Institute, New Delhi for their cooperation all through. My special thanks to library staff for their patient help in carrying out the project. My thanks to Ms Nazia Ansari, Ms. Samreen, and Ms. Satyabhama from Indian Social Institute for their patient help in typing work and data entry work into SPSS software. I must acknowledge various field level agencies, government departments, health institutions and websites for providing data and information to carry out the project successfully.

Dr Archana Sinha

Department of Women's Studies,

Indian Social Institute, New Delhi

Glossary of Abbreviations

AHS - Annual Health Survey

ANC - Anti Natal Care

ANM - Auxiliary Nurse Midwife

APL - Above Poverty Line

ASHA - Accredited Social Health Activist

AWW - Angan Wadi Worker

AYUS - Adarsh Yuva Samiti

AYUSH - Ayurveda Yoga Unani Siddha and Homeopathy

BAMS - Bachelor of Ayurvedic Medicine and Surgery

BPL - Below Poverty Line

CHC - Community Health Centre

CSSM - Child Survival and Safe Motherhood

DRS - Development and Research Services

EAG - Empowered Action Group

FRUs - First Referral Units

GP - Gram Panchayat

HMIS - Health Management Information Systems

HPS - High Performing States

ICPD - International Conference on Population and Development

IFA - Iron Folic Acid

IMR - Infant Mortality Rate

IPHS	-	Indian Public Health Standard
JSY	-	Janani Suraksha Yojana
LPS	-	Low Performing State
MCH	-	Maternal and Child Health
MDG	-	Millennium Development Goal
MMR	-	Maternal Mortality Rate
MoHFW	-	Ministry of Health and Family Welfare
MPW	-	Multi Purpose Worker
NFHS	-	National Family Health Survey
NMBS	-	National Maternity Benefit Scheme
NRHM	-	National Rural Health Mission
NSAP	-	National Social Assistance Programme
NSHRC	-	National Health Systems Resource Centre
NSSO	-	National Sample Survey Organisation
OBC	-	Other Backward Caste
OT	-	Operation Theatre
PHS	-	Public Health Service
PNC	-	Post Natal Care
PSU	-	Primary Sample Unit
RCH	-	Reproductive and Child Health
RHS	-	Reproductive Health Specialist
RMP	-	Registered Medical Practitioner
SC	-	Scheduled Caste; Sub Centre
SPSS	-	Statistical Package of Social Science
SRS	-	Sample Registration System
ST	-	Scheduled Tribe
TBA	-	Trained Birth Attendant

TT - Tetanus Toxoid

UNFPA - United Nations Population Fund

UNICEF - United Nations Children's Fund

WHO - World Health Organisation

Chapter - 1

Understanding Maternal Health Care in India

Maternal health issues continue to remain important in national health policies. Institutions such as WHO, UNICEF and UNFPA had reported that India accounts for a third of maternal deaths worldwide (KLP, 2009). One-fourth of the world's unattended deliveries take place here, and India by itself records 22 per cent of pregnancy-related deaths worldwide, and extremely low percentage of institutional deliveries is one of its major concerns. Amid those women belonging to below poverty line and living in remote villages, the number of institutional deliveries is almost negligible. Helping mothers' lives is not only of moral essence, but this also benefits their children. There is also a relationship between maternal health and Millennium Development Goals, such as eradicating extreme poverty, and reducing child mortality. As per Baqui, et al (2007), in India, 75.3 per cent of all births in rural areas occur at home. Largely, this is due to the fact that the expenses in institutional deliveries are much higher as compared to that in home deliveries. Even in public health facilities, average expenditure incurred is reported to be as high as Rs. 882 even for the below poverty level households. Practically, one-third of the total expenditure was incurred in purchasing medicines and other diagnostic services from outside and one-fourth on transportation (GOR, 2007).

Maternal mortality has a range of underlying determinants, including social, economical, cultural, geographical, and health system factors. It is defined as the death of a woman while pregnant or within 42 days of termination of pregnancy, regardless of the site or duration of pregnancy from any cause related to or aggravated by the pregnancy or its management (UNICEF, 2009). Maternal death represents the most extreme outcome; however as per an estimate for each woman who dies an estimated 20 more suffer from infection, injury and disability connected to pregnancy or childbirth (Singh et al., 2009). India contribute almost one third of total maternal deaths in the world. The annual maternal death toll in India is controversial but it stands somewhere in between 63000 to 117000 (Singh et al, 2009; SRS, 2011). According to World Health Organization (2005) approximately 80 per cent of the maternal deaths globally occur due to haemorrhage, sepsis, unsafe induced abortion, hypertensive disorder of pregnancy and obstructed labour. These deaths can be avoided by providing effective and timely maternal health care (World Vision, 2008). Right from the turn of twenty first century India has shown remarkable progress in reducing maternal death. Sample Registration Survey of India has reported decline in MMR from 327 in year 1999-2001 to 212 in year 2007-09 (SRS, 2011). However the decreased maternal mortality rate of 212 represents maternal death of 63000 women every year. UNICEF report on coverage evaluation reveals tremendous increase in women's accessibility of health institutions in rural India for institutional delivery. The report claims increase in institutional delivery from 39.7 per cent in 2005 to 69 per cent in 2009 (UNICEF, 2009). On the other hand various government documents/statistics reveal that there is huge shortage of health institutions and health professionals in India.

Within India a wide disparity exists in maternal mortality outcome of different states. The MMR ranges from 95 in Kerala to 480 in Assam. Empowered Action Group (EAG) states (Bihar Chhattisgarh, Jharkhand, Orissa, U.P, Uttarakhand, Rajasthan, and Madhya Pradesh) have worst maternal health outcome. These states have shown slower progress in last one decade even after having high national focus through NRHM/JSY. EAG states share around 48 per cent of total women of India and has 61 per cent of share in total maternal death of India (SRS, 2011). Maternal mortality rate of these states is as high as 380. In the first decade of the 21st century many progressing states especially southern states of India have succeeded in decreasing MMR by 38 per cent. EAG state showed comparatively slower progress in same time period. These states showed a decline of 33 per cent in MMR during first decade of twenty first century (SRS, 2011). All these data and statistics on maternal health are highly relevant at this point of time when nationally and internationally several targets are set to reduce maternal mortality. Fifth Millennium Development Goal (MDG) had the commitment to enhance maternal health by reducing MMR up to 109 in India by the end of year 2015. National Rural Health Mission (NRHM) had far ambitious target to reduce MMR up to 100 by the end of year 2012. Data on maternal mortality rate does not represent complete picture of maternal health, however these data gives us indication about status of maternal health. Maternal health in totality has to do much beyond these statistics.

India introduced maternal health services through Family Planning and Maternal and Child Health Programme in 1950s. As a responsible nation it has a track record in following international policies and trajectory addressing global maternal health concerns. In response to the safe motherhood inititiave-1987, anchored by UNICEF, UNFPA, World Bank, WHO, IPPF and Population Council, India shifted its strategy on antenatal care, risk approach for detection or complications and training of TBAs. With the launch of the Child Survival and Safe Motherhood (CSSM) Programme in 1992 government of India committed towards universalizing maternal care and enhancing institutional capacity to cater the needs of essential obstetric care. Up to 1990s maternal health was a part of targeted Family Planning Programme in India, which had prime focus to stabilize population. International conference on Population and Development (ICPD) at Cairo in 1994 and fourth World conference on Women in Beijing in 1995 provided new direction to maternal health approach of India. Following the trajectory of these international commitments, India broaden its scope by involving men's participation, incorporating adolescent reproductive and sexual health, introducing Reproductive and Child Health (RCH) Programme and adopted target-free approach to family planning. Government of India launched National Rural Health Mission (NRHM) in 2005 to provide accessible, affordable, and quality health care to rural populations, especially vulnerable and underserved population groups in the Country. Janani Suraksha Yojana (JSY) is a safe motherhood intervention under the National Rural Health Mission of Government of India. This scheme implemented in all Indian states and Union Territories, with a special focus on Low Performing States (LPS). In April 2005, Janani Suraksha Yojana was initiated by modifying the National Maternity Benefit Scheme (NMBS), which was initiated way back in 1995 as one of the components of the National Social Assistance Programme (NSAP). The National Maternity Benefit Scheme (NMBS) was transferred from the Ministry of Rural Development to the Department of Health and Family Welfare during the year 2001-02. The NMBS provides for financial assistance of Rs. 500 per birth up to two live births to the pregnant women who have attained 19 years of age and belong to the below poverty line (BPL) households. Improvement in maternal health is one of its focus area with specific, time bound and measurable outcome approach. Reducing MMR to 100 deaths per 100000 live births by 2012 is one of the goals of NRHM. Janani Suraksha Yojana (JSY) is adopted as a specific scheme of NRHM to address the issues of maternal health.

When Janani Suraksha Yojana was launched, the financial assistance of Rs. 500, which was offered uniformly throughout the country to BPL pregnant women under NMBS, was substituted by graded scale of support based on the classification of States as well as whether beneficiary was from rural/urban areas. States were classified into 'Low Performing States' and 'High Performing States' according to the institutional delivery rate, that is to say, states having institutional delivery 25 per cent or less were termed as Low Performing States (LPS) and those which have institutional delivery rate more than 25 per cent were classified as High Performing States (HPS). Some of the states having high fertility and mortality have been termed as Empowered Action Group (EAG) states. In India, cultural standards and principles promote early marriage of women in EAG states that are behind in terms of women's reproductive and child health in relationship to other states. The rural poor women, who are not well nourished and have early pregnancy, would augment the risk of unsafe pregnancy outcomes. To combat the difficulty Janani Suraksha Yojana (JSY), a safe motherhood intervention promotes institutional delivery.

In accordance to this Uttarakhand is classified as one among the eight erstwhile EAG states as a Low Performing State, and thus JSY has been implemented.

1.1 Socio-Demographic Influences and Maternal Health

Health care seeking behaviour is much rooted in social construction of community. Digambar et al. (2011) categorizes influencing factors of maternal health utilization into individual, household, and community levels. Depending on the indicator of maternal health services, the relevant determinates vary. Singh, et al. (2005) found low level of education and low status of women in society prevents them from taking antenatal care even if the services are available. This study of rural women looked into various cross cutting factors affecting women health. It reveals several social and demographical factors such as high work load, lack of sanitation, occupational health and gender base differences leads to poor health of women. Higher dependency on quacks or RMP even for reproductive health resulted in delivery complications like septic, uterine rapture, perennial tear, tetanus etc.

Srinivasan et al. (2006) summarized an operational research project on maternal and child health in Karnataka with government program that, morbidity and mortality levels of mother and children can be reduced by providing maternal and child health care to all mother. Study reveals that working mothers and mothers with higher birth order are experiencing less safe deliveries and availing inadequate ANC services. Education of mothers is significant to increase attitude of availing ANC services and safe deliveries.

Social and medical causes of maternal deaths are highlighted by Haralkar et al. (2012) in a study of maternal death in a tertiary care hospital of Maharashtra found that more than half of deaths occur during post natal period. And maternal mortality risk is high among young women below 20 years of age. Study further discuss that the problem lies in poor general condition of women, rapid succession of unsupervised pregnancies, ignorance, and lack of timely medical care.

Chauhan et al. (2012) explored socio-demographic determinants of institutional and safe delivery in Hanumangarh district of Rajasthan.

Logistic regression analysis of first hand collected data reveals that religion, female education, husband's occupation, household income, and birth order are important predictors of safe delivery. On the contrary caste is not significantly associated with safe delivery. Study also reveals that among all institutional deliveries share of respondents belong to SCs is highest. The cash incentive of Janani Suraksha Yojana might attract poor population belonging to SCs. On the contrary percentage of deliveries at private hospitals has been found lowest among SCs. Study associate this result with many other issues like accessibility, customs and affordability to bear the cost of health care services.

A similar study in Philippines by Rogen et al. (2004) analyzing MCH 2002 data of Philippines attempted to identify the factors affecting Maternal Health Utilization in Philippines. The study has compared several socio-demographic characteristics of Filipino women with prenatal care, delivery care and post natal care outcomes of Philippines. Study found that education of mother, work status, age, and rural-urban location as significant and independent predictors for the use of MCH services in Philippines.

Sahu et al. (2012) have examined the knowledge and utilization of JSY among slum dwellers of Raipur city in Chhattisgarh. A large sample size of this study resides in one kilometer radius of B.R. Ambedkar Memorial Hospital in Raipur. Study observes that utilization of antenatal services is better but postnatal services were poorly utilized even by those who availed the scheme. Study concludes that lack of community awareness is responsible for low level of utilization of post natal care even after easy accessible health institution.

Kundu, (2010) using data of NFHS-II, III and NSSO (2006) analyzed social and geographical determinants of utilization of health care in India. Study identified attitude towards the health condition, women's lack of control over household resources, less power in decision making, women's care giving role, lack of autonomy and low level of education, less exposure to mass media, and less access to money and mobility as key social factors are influential to women's access to health care. It reveals that when women have lower access to maternal health care services, the risk of maternal and child mortality will increase. Similarly, vulnerability and risk in children increases if MMR increases. The NFHS-III data study revealed that the cause of women not receiving antenatal care in the rural area is that the male head did not think it was necessary. The second important reason in high cost of hospitalization and third cause is the health facility is too far or there is no suitable transport to travel to the facility.

Apart from several studies on socio-demographic factors, Singh et al. (2010) conducted a similar study in relation to accessibility of ASHA under NRHM. This study was conducted in rural area of Lucknow district to identify factors those affect utilization of services of ASHAs under NRHM in relation to maternal health. Study concluded that education of women, higher socio-economic status of family, younger age of mother and Hindu as compared to Muslim are more likely to utilize ASHAs services. Contrary to NFHS, the study found women from schedule caste group avail more services of antenatal and post natal care.

Wide range of literature is available on social and demographic determinants of maternal health care utilization. There is complex relation between influential socio-demographic variables and health care which needs to be explored with a multi-dimensional paradigm in order to challenge pure technocratic medical approach of health policy formation (Nayar 2007, Bir 2006). A detail study in this matter within the framework of JSY helps to understand how such factors were taken in consideration while implementation of Janani Suraksha Yojana.

1.2 Recognizing Maternal Health Care System

Maternal health is a globally accepted important human development indicator. International community, recognizes maternal well being as basic human right of women. Through various conventions United Nation Organisation has tried to make member states responsible for providing quality health care to its citizen. Even after number of international commitments and constitutional provision, safe motherhood is not guaranteed in practice to the citizens in India (CRR 2008). India contributes nearly one quarter of total maternal deaths in the world. As per an estimate of World Health

Organization annually 1, 17,000 women die during pregnancy period in this country (Singh, et.al 2009). The accurate calculation of maternal deaths in India is difficult due to inappropriate reporting mechanism and lack of health system in rural areas. Among the available data on maternal mortality ratio shows the wide spread disparities among different states of India ranges from 81 in Kerala to 390 in Assam (SRS 2011). The huge number of maternal deaths in India is further supported by insufficient public health service delivery. More than 36 per cent of women are dependent on traditional birth attendants for their deliveries. Only 40 per cent women have access to institutional deliveries. Similarly, poor access to antenatal, and postnatal care increases risk of mother during delivery period (NFHS-III).

In India maternal health was highlighted in the recommendations of the Bhore Committee in 1946. (Bannerji 1985). As a result from the 1950s, India had a Family Planning and Maternal and Child Health Programme (Khanna et al, 2012). Maternal health policies in India since then revised, revisited and re-directed as per need and understanding of different time period (Soman, 1998). The changes in polices were done at every level such as approach, understanding, implementation and resource allocation to ensure safe motherhood. Janani Suraksha Yojana is the latest and unique maternal health programme that provides minimum quality maternal health services to pregnant women in India (MoHFW). The NRHM invests in improving public sector facilities in terms of infrastructure, human resource and skill to ensure availability and quality of health system for health services including JSY (Khanna, et al, 2012).

Even after the implementation of several policies and programmes, maternal death remains high in India. As per an analysis of Sample Registration System of India, maternal mortality ratio has declined from 398 in 1998 to 212 in 2009. In high focus states of NRHM (that is, EAG states and Assam) declined in maternal mortality is much slower as compare to other states. These states recorded 33 per cent decline in year 2007-09 as compared to year 1999-2001 while southern states recorded 38 per cent of decline in maternal death in same time period (SRS 2011).

India's failure in ensuring safe motherhood to pregnant women even after such a wide range of programmes and policies is a big concern. Several quick track initiatives in the past have failed to deliver effective health services in India (Rao 1998). The maternal well being or effectiveness of any maternal health programme depends on a rage of underlying determinants including social, cultural, health system and economic factors (Khanna, et al 2012). United Nation's Treaty Monitoring Bodies have specifically highlighted India's failure to uphold its obligation. They consistently expressed concern about high maternal death as a consequences of lack of access to appropriate maternal health care services and the poor quality of care that undermine the safety of institutional delivery (CRR 2008, Shariff, et al 2002). It is evident from number of studies that apart from social, economical and demographic factors, accessibility and quality of health facilities are obstacles in achieving the goal of safe motherhood (CRR 2008, Khanna et al 2012).

Number of the studies around the globe investigated patterns of health service utilization and factors affecting them. To study utilization pattern of JSY services and factors affecting them, it is important to understand maternal health in broader framework in India. The present report is structured into six chapters, including the present one. The first chapter discusses the methodology of the study and provides details of the study design, sample size, sampling procedure and coverage of different types of respondents in the selected state of Uttarakhand. While programmatic and financial management of the JSY scheme towards safe institutional delivery is presented in chapter two, the chapter three talks about health status scenario of Uttarakhand in terms of health indicators and institutions. In chapter four, discussion is made on the findings from the assessment wherein awareness and utilisation of the JSY programme, uptake of ante-natal, delivery, and post-natal care services, quality of care at the three levels of institutions as perceived by the mothers who delivered in an institution during the reference year and receipt of benefits under the JSY scheme along with problems faced are presented. Further, chapter five, highlights the service providers' awareness and experience about the JSY scheme, their role and performance and issues related to their receipt of JSY payment are dealt with. The last chapter six, provides key findings, recommendations and conclusions for strengthening the JSY programme.

1.3 Contextual Framework

It is observed that high rate of maternal mortality, morbidity and a large number of unsafe deliveries are a few key indicators of vulnerability of women, particularly for the mothers. Janani Suraksha Yojana (JSY), a flagship component of NRHM, was introduced in 2005 with the objective of reducing maternal and child mortality by promoting and strengthening institutional care during entire pregnancy period, and this program is carrying best practices from the lessons learned in the past (Lahariya 2009). Even after seven years of implementation of this ambitious programme, maternal health outcomes are not satisfactory to the level of its pre-designed target for year 2012. NRHM had the target to reduce MMR to 100 in Uttarakhand by the end of 2012. But the annual health survey (2011) conducted by Registrar General of India reported MMR as high as 188 in the state. Utilization of health services is defined in numerous ways in health research. Behavioral model of health service use, defines "types and frequency of care consumption" as utilization of health services. However, World Health Organization defines utilization as "experience of people to their receipt of health care services of different type". These two definitions provide qualitative and quantitative aspects of actual use of services. The quantity and quality of actual use of services lies in various dimensions of access to health care. Often access is used to describe characteristics influencing the initial contact or use of services and providers. WHO defines access to health care as, "population's ease in reaching health services" A comprehensive conceptualization of access to health care in relation to utilization by Levesque et al[1], defines various dimensions of access as ability of population and outreach of systems. They broadly categorizes the dimensions into five categories i.e. personal empowerment of people, availability of services, outreach of system, acceptability of services, and affordability of people. Access to health care has been defined in numerous ways in health research depending upon definer's view and hence there is no consensus on definition and dimensions of access.

Explanation of access by Levesque et al includes dimensions that interface between the social, demographical, economical, and environmental context of community to health systems and service providers. These dimensions can be adopted to study the access of maternal health services of Janani Suraksha Yojana, with selected features of each dimension as per the requirement and scope of the project. Dimensions of access to maternal health services of JSY in relation to utilization are thus modified as follows for the requirement and scope of the present study (refer framework). The first dimension is awareness that builds care seeking behaviour in community. Second is availability of health services and providers to cater to the needs of population. Third dimension is physical accessibility of services that ease in terms of time and comfort. Fourth is acceptability of care among population that involves social values and norms concerning health care and belief. The fifth dimension is affordability of services that involves cost of service and affordability of population to use them. Further, dimensions of the access affecting the maternal health care are also linked with various social-cultural and economical variables (refer framework, Figure: 1.1). These variables influence to a great extent, dimensions of the access affecting the maternal health care services bringing disparities in health outcome observed at various levels.

1.4 Conceptual Framework

The study investigates causes behind high level of MMR in the sample districts even after implementation of Janani Suraksha Yojana for more than seven years. This will help in finding out factors that hinder Janani Suraksha Yojana (JSY) in achieving the goal of safe motherhood in the state of Uttarakhand. Uttarakhand is one of the high focus states of National Rural Health Mission (2005-2012) due to its poor health scenario. It is observed that high rate of maternal mortality, morbidity and a large number of unsafe deliveries are a few key indicators of vulnerability of women, particularly for the mothers. The mission had a target to reduce MMR to 100 in Uttarakhand by the end of 2012. But the annual health survey (2011) conducted by Registrar General of India reported MMR as high as 188 in the state. With this framework, the study investigates causes behind high level

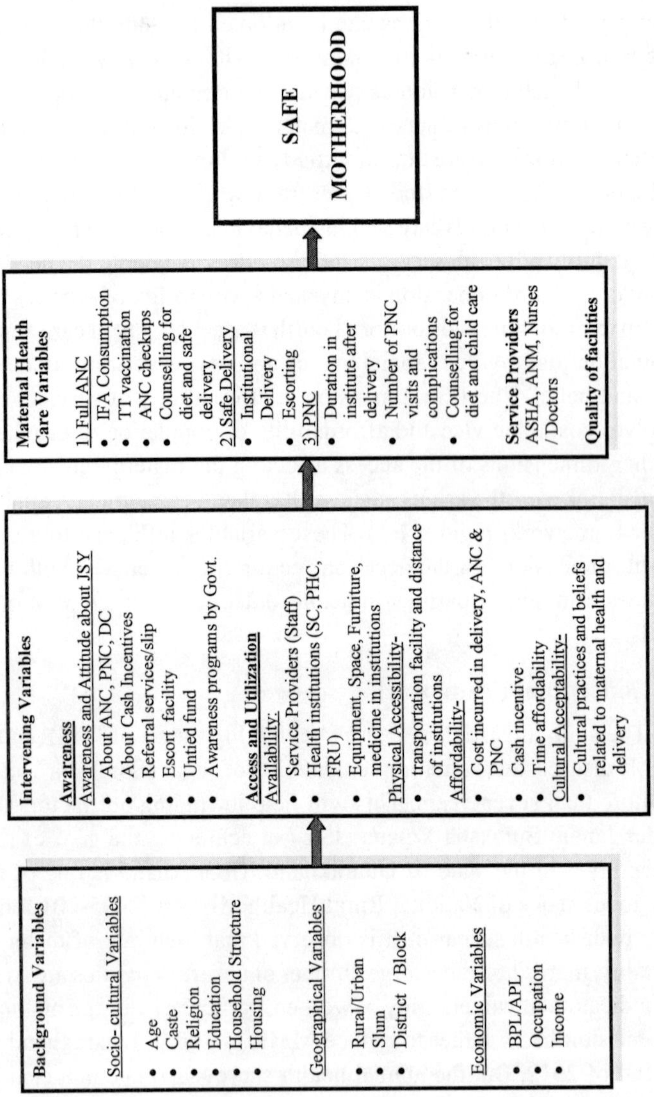

Figure 1.1: Maternal Health Care: A Study of Janani Suraksha Yojana in Two Districts of Uttarakhand: A Framework

of MMR in the sample districts even after implementation of Janani Suraksha Yojana for more than seven years. And thus finds out factors that hinder Janani Suraksha Yojana (JSY) in achieving goal of safe motherhood in the state of Uttarakhand. It is an attempt to pool resources, reducing regional imbalance in health infrastructure, community participation and ownership, and meeting Indian Public Health Standards in each block of the country.

With this framework, the study investigates causes behind high level of MMR in the selected districts of Almora and Haridwar which have been implementing Janani Suraksha Yojana for more than seven years.

1.5 Objectives of the Study

The present study attempts to explore institutional and societal dimensions that affect in access to and utilization of maternal health care services in the state of Uttarakhand.

- To survey the status of human and infrastructural resources and services provided by SC, PHC, and CHC to promote institutional maternal health care.
- To study different dimensions of access to and utilization of maternal health care services.
- To study the relationship between social, economical, cultural, and geographical variables and access to and utilization of maternal health care services.
- To study the status and functioning of ASHA / ANM and other health providers in promoting institutional care / delivery
- To make recommendations for effective implementation of JSY.

1.6 Study Area

Uttarakhand is a newly formed state, carved out of the former Uttar Pradesh in the year 2000. It is largely a hilly State. The state is comprised of 13 districts, of these 13 districts, two districts (Haridwar and Udham Singh Nagar) are entirely situated in plain; two districts (Nainital and Dehradun) have large areas in the plains, whereas the other nine districts comprise the hill region of the state. The hill region is less developed in terms of infrastructure such as road, electricity, school, hospital, communication etc. The inequality in infrastructure leads to increasing disparity in terms of socio-economic development between the hills and the plains. Assuring basic need such as health, education, transportation, communication, food is always a challenge in hill districts (Figure: 1.2).

Figure 1.2: Uttarakhand Map with Districts Almora and Haridwar

Eleven hill and semi hill districts of Uttarakhand shares more than 68 per cent of state population dependent on mountain agriculture and livestock for their livelihood. As an impact of new economic policies, these occupations are not economically viable at this point of time, so it is resulting massive migration in search of job from hilly districts. The un-productive traditional occupations and lack of infrastructure for development leads to further marginalization of people in this region. In the plain districts (Udham Singh Nagar and Haridwar) population density is much higher than other districts of Uttarakhand. All big cities of the state are located in these districts; with the formation of new state these cities attracted major private and public development initiatives (Table: 1.1).

Table 1.1: Population Profile of Uttarakhand

Geography	*District*	*Total Population*	*Total SC Population*	*Total ST Population*
Hills	Almora	632866	140430	878
	Bageshwar	247163	64524	1943
	Chamoli	370359	67539	10484
	Champawat	224542	38098	740
	Garhwal	697078	106653	1594
	Pithoragarh	462289	106449	19279
	Rudraprayag	227439	40311	186
	Tehri Garhwal	604747	87325	691
	Uttarkashi	295013	67467	2685
Semi-Hills	Dehradun	1282143	173448	99329
	Nainital	762909	148184	4961
Plains	Udham Singh Nagar	1235614	162782	110220
	Haridwar	1447187	313976	3139
	TOTAL	8489349	1517186	256129

Source: Census, 2001.

1.7 Methodology

This section describes the study design, sample size, sampling procedure and coverage of different categories of respondents including the beneficiaries in the selected state of Uttarakhand, which is one of the high focus states of National Rural Health Mission (2005-2012) due to its poor health scenario. The study has looked into the broad trends of maternal health care situation and various factors affecting maternal health care in selected district. It has used both qualitative and quantitative techniques in the selected districts Almora and Haridwar.

- Case study method is used to understand the impact of JSY at different levels.
- Primary data related to maternal care, accessibility of health institutions and JSY care, and basic social, economical, geographical and demographic information were gathered from the study areas–through interview schedules at beneficiary level as well as level of service providers of JSY care.
- Secondary data related to implementation and impact of JSY are/were gathered in the selected area using data sources,

such as–Census, NFHS (National Family Health Survey), AHS (Annual Health Survey), DLHS-III (District Level Health Survey), RHS (Rural Health Statistics–2011), NRHM-MIS.

- Statistical Package to Social Science (SPSS) was utilized to process primary data gathered from beneficiary and service provider. It was also utilize to analyze data and run basic statistical test.

1.8 Data Collection Tools

The "Interview schedule" and "case study" were used for beneficiary women as well as for the officials at the levels of Sub-Centre, primary health centre, and community health centre. The following three sets of questionnaires/interview schedules were used:

1st at Beneficiary level schedule

2nd at Service Provider level schedule (Sub-Centre level, PHC, CHC, and District hospital)

3rd at health facility level schedule (to generate profile of SC, PHC, CHC and DH especially from maternal health care point of view)

1.9 Sample Selection

For the survey of beneficiaries of JSY, the study adopted a four stage sampling design with selection of the districts, block (rural)/ city (urban), village (rural)/ward (urban) and respondents towards selection of the target sample size of the mothers in Uttarakhand. It has adopted purposive and proportionate to population sampling methodology in order to bring out the ground reality of the maternal health care of JSY under NRHM. The sampling procedure to select the sample is described below:

- Selection of Districts

In the first stage sampling, all districts of Uttarakhand were categorized in hill and plain areas. Purposively one district from Hill (that is, Almora) and one district from Plain (that is, Haridwar) were selected based on their highest SC population.

- Selection of Block and City

Second stage sampling procedure comprises selection of rural and urban locations in the selected district of Uttarakhand. Keeping geographical disparities in mind from each district, one block nearest to District Hospital and another block farthest from District Hospital were selected. Similarly to collect information from urban beneficiary one city closest to District Hospital and another city farthest from District Hospital were selected.

- Selection of Primary Sample Unit for Rural/Urban Area

In the third stage of sampling primary sample units for rural and urban locations were selected. Gram Panchayat (GP) for rural and City Ward (CW) for urban locations are defined as primary sample unit (PSU). Purposively Gram Panchayats (GPs) in each block with ample availability of Schedule Caste (SC) population were shortlisted. Ample is defined as availability of SC population between 30 to 50 per cent of total population. This criterion helped to get substantial availability of respondents from SCs/non-SC categories. Randomly few Gram Panchayats among the shortlisted GPs were selected as Primary Sample Unit (PSU). The number of sample GPs vary in each district due to wide disparities in population size of GPs and Crude Birth Rate (CBR) in selected districts.

In the same manner, purposively City Wards (CWs) in each city with ample availability of Schedule Caste (SC) population were shortlisted. This criterion helped to get substantial availability of respondent from SCs / non-SC category. Randomly two City Wards among the shortlisted Wards were selected as Primary Sample Unit (PSU).

- Respondents' Selection

The fourth state of sampling deals with selection of respondents. All the women who attained motherhood between 1st April 2012 to 31st March 2013 in the selected villages and city wards were listed (as respondents) towards sample selection. ASHA and AWW of respective primary sample unit were contacted to prepare authentic list of mothers. Randomly respondents of JSY beneficiary were selected for interview from the list of eligible respondents in both rural and urban area.

- Selection of Service Provider and Health Institutions

The Service providers are often accessed by respondents of JSY beneficiary such as ASHA, ANM and Doctors at PHC and CHC were interviewed. Mostly these service providers are from the public health institutions located in selected village/ward or close to the selected village and ward. A profile of all such public health institutions is captured through a separate survey questionnaire. Mostly the head of the institution were interviewed for the same.

The service providers included the following.

- Accredited Social Health Activist (ASHA)
- Auxiliary Nurse Midwife (ANM)
- ICDS worker (AWW)
- Doctors at PHC and CHC frequently referred to or accessed by target beneficiary
- Other staff of health institution associated with maternal health care service

1.10 Sample Size

- There were three hundred and thirteen (313) mothers and nearly forty (40) service providers were selected from rural and urban primary sample units. Sample of respondent mothers is divided among sample districts in proportion to their population size and their share in total population of state. Population-wise Haridwar district is 2.30 times higher than Almora, so sample size of Haridwar is 2.30 times larger than Almora (Table: 1.2).
- Further the division of rural and urban sampling in each district is/were proportionate to the rural-urban population of respective district.
- Around 40 service providers were selected from both districts together.

Table 1.2: Sample Distribution in Uttarakhand

District	*Total Population (Census-2001)*	*Share in total population of Uttarakhand*	*Rural population (Census-2001)*	*Urban population (Census-2001*	*Sample of Respondent Mothers*		
					Rural	*Urban*	*Total*
Almora	630,567	7.45%	576,062 (91%)	54,505 (9%)	93	10	103
Hardwar	1,447,187	17%	1,000,912 (69%)	446,275 (31%)	143	67	210
Total	2,077,754		1,576,974 (76%)	500,780 (24%)	236	77	313

(Figures in brackets indicate total share of rural and urban population in selected districts)

Chapter - 2

Promoting Safe Institutional Delivery

In India, nearly 56,000 women die every year due to pregnancy related complications. Likewise, every year more than 13 lac infants die within first year of the birth and out of these nearly two-third of the infant deaths (that is, nine lacs) take place within the first month of their birth. Further, of these, nearly three-fourth (that is, 7 lacs) of the deaths take place within first week of their birth and then a majority of these happen within two days of birth. Hence, in order to reduce the maternal and infant mortality, Reproductive and Child Health Programme (RCH) under the National Rural Health Mission is being put into practice to promote institutional deliveries so that skilled attendants at birth are available and women and new born can be saved from pregnancy related deaths. Janani Suraksha Yojana (JSY) is a key intervention that has led to an increase in institutional deliveries. This chapter deals with the programmatic and financial management of the Janani Suraksha Yojana scheme towards safe institutional delivery.

2.1 Understanding Janani Suraksha Yojana (JSY)

The National Rural Health Mission (NRHM), launched by Government of India in 2005 with the vision of recognizing the importance of health in the process of economic and social development and improving the quality of life of people. NRHM is meant to provide assured, responsive and quality health services to the poor and needy. It is also supposed to address the health needs of women on a priority basis. The Mission seeks to provide accessible, affordable and quality health care to rural populations, especially vulnerable and underserved population groups in the country. The main approach of NRHM is to improve public health sector facilities in terms of infrastructure, human resource and skill to ensure availability and quality of health system for its different focused health programme including Janani Suraksha Yojana. The mission attempts to improve public health facilities by upgrading them as per the norms of Indian Public Health Standard (IPHS).

Janani Suraksha Yojana is a special and focused scheme under National Rural Health Mission (NRHM). Government of India introduced Janani Suraksha Yojana (JSY) on 12th April 2005 with the objective of reducing the maternal and infant mortality by promoting institutional deliveries. JSY is 100 per cent centrally sponsored scheme which, integrate the cash assistance with antenatal care during the pregnancy period, institutional care during delivery, and immediate post-partum period in a health centre by establishing a system of coordinated care by field level health worker. The JSY scheme is modified replacement of National Maternity Benefit Scheme (NMBS). Under this new version a detailed system is developed to track pregnant women for each service during pregnancy, during delivery and after delivery with a time line to deliver the services and ensure efficient implementation. More than one crore women are reported being benefitted from the scheme annually. This new initiative provides completely free and cashless services to pregnant women including normal deliveries and c-section operations and sick newborns (up to 30 days after birth) at public health institutions in both rural and urban areas. The cashless and free entitlements for pregnant women under Janani Suraksha Yojana include- free and cashless delivery; free C-Section; free drugs and consumables; free diagnostics; free diet during stay in the health institutions; free provision of blood; exemption from user charges; free transport from home to health institutions; free transport between facilities in case of referral; and free drop back from institutions to home after two days of stay. The main features of this scheme includes- free and no expense delivery, as well as caesarean section entitled to all pregnant women delivering in public health institutions. The entitlements include free medicines, free diet up to 3 days during normal delivery and up to 7 days for C-section, free check-ups, and free blood wherever vital. This program also offers for free transport from home to institution, between facilities in case of a referral and drop back home. The Yojana has identified ASHA (Accredited Social Health Activist) as an effective link between the Government and poor pregnant women in ten low performing states namely eight EAG (Empowered Action Group) states and Assam and Jammu & Kashmir. ASHA has a role to link pregnant women with public health facilities for maternal care.

Table 2.1: Eligibility Criteria of JSY Target Group

Category of States	*Rural Area*			*Urban Area*		
	Mother's Package	*ASHA's Package*	*Total Assistance*	*Mother's Package*	*ASHA's Package*	*Total*
LPS	Rs. 1400	Rs. 600	Rs. 2000	Rs. 1000	Rs. 200	Rs. 1200
HPS	Rs. 700	Rs. 200	Rs. 900	Rs. 600	Rs. 200	Rs. 800

JSY is safe motherhood scheme launched by Government of India; it is not just limited to cash assistance to the pregnant women but it also includes following:

- Early registration of the beneficiary with the help of the village level health workers like ASHA or an equivalent worker.
- Early identification of complicated cases.
- Providing at least three antenatal care, conducting deliveries and post delivery visits.
- Organizing appropriate referral and providing referral transport to the pregnant mother;
- Convergence with Integrated Child Development Services (ICDS) worker by way of involving Anganwadi worker (AWW) intensively.
- Devising as well as ensuring transparent and timely disbursement of the cash assistance to the mother and the incentive to the Accredited Social Health Activist (ASHA) or an equivalent worker with fund available with ANM.

- Operationalization of 24/7 delivery services at PHC level to provide basic obstetric care,
- Operationalization of First Referral Units (FRUs) to provide emergency obstetric care,
- Building partnerships through a process of recognition/ accreditation with doctors, hospitals/nursing homes/clinics from the private sector especially in the rural areas to provide obstetric services to the JSY beneficiary. States/UTs have been classified into two categories based on the institutional delivery rate. The ten states namely the eight EAG (Empowered Action Group) states and the states of Assam and Jammu & Kashmir would constitute Low Performing States (LPS) and the rest High Performing States (HPS).
- Initially the target group of JSY were women from BPL families and were eligible for the benefit only up to two deliveries. After October 2006 all eligibility criteria were removed and all women who gave birth to new borne children/witnessed deliveries at health institutions are provided monetary incentives in the LPS states as follows **(Table 2.1).**

2.2 Health System and Service Providers

The recent studies have acknowledged improper implementation of NRHM strategies. Planning Commission (2011) in its broad based evaluation of NRHM in seven different low performing states of India reveals state specific results. Study reveals that Institutional deliveries in almost all the seven states depict quantum jump from 2005-06 to 2008-09. Study reveals that even till 2009 the speed of up gradation of health facilities such as DH, SDH, CHC, PHC and SC according to IPHS is not up to mark. The shortage of medical and paramedical staff in CHCs, PHCs and SCs hampers preparedness to deliver quality care. PHC functioning on 24x7 bases seems to be proportionately quite low in almost all the seven states. Shortage of ambulances and mobile health units are also hampering the outreach of health care services. Women delivering new born babies also don't stay for minimum 48 hours after delivery because of lacking basic facilities like cleanliness, electricity, potable water etc.

Issues related to health system and service providers are also highlighted by Mavalankar et al. (2009) in a research based on several secondary data sets. Study identified several logistic and infrastructural lacunas in providing quality health care in the state of Gujarat. The study reveals lack of managerial capacity, shortage of skilled human resources, non-availability of blood in rural areas and infrastructural and supply bottleneck as key challenges in reducing maternal mortality ratio in Gujarat. Highlighting issues related to service delivery system in maternal health care study identified problems of inadequate infrastructure and equipment, shortage of human resources, lack of supplies, and inadequate monitoring and supervision in different level of public health institutions. Health professionals do not like to stay in rural areas because of lack of infrastructure and quality of life. And a socio-political milieu strongly functions which encourages lack of accountability. Study also pointed towards lack of skilled birth attendants in health institutions like PHC, SC and CHC. Study found that the staff nurses and LHVs at the PHCs and CHCs are not adequately skilled to provide delivery care. Medical officers posted at PHCs are not skilled for delivery care and basic EmOC.

Health statistics reveals poor health system in India (RHS 2011). Concurrent evaluation of NRHM in year 2008-09 by MoHFW found insufficient infrastructure and poor quality of services in different low performing states including Uttarakhand. PHCs are primary health providing facilities in rural area but in Uttarakhand only 25 per cent PHCs are functioning on 24x7 bases. More than 42 per cent PHCs even don't have functional labour room (MoHFW 2009). Objective of safe motherhood cannot be achieved without effective health facilities. Sharma, (2008) in his early evaluation of JSY in two districts of Rajasthan assessed logistic arrangement required for the effective implementation of JSY. The study found that government of Rajasthan is still in its way to arrange resources such as human resource and establishing desired financial system. Though evaluation conducted after two years of JSY implementation it tells less about impact. But it highlights low level of awareness both among beneficiary and stakeholder about community participation in implementation of JSY such as provision of village health committee.

Lack of coordination in JSY and NRHM has led to problems such as over burden in health institutions. My-Heart (2010) in a study commissioned by Planning Commission of India attempted to map maternal death in Orissa. Study reveals that the maximum maternal deaths occur during post natal period due to lack of services. Least importance is given to the mother in case of post partum period complications. Study reveals that introduction of JSY has increased pressure of high level of institutional deliveries. But the institutions don't have enough bed and other facilities to retain women after delivery. Studies on health system effectiveness in relation of JSY and NRHM found slow progress in building infrastructure and arranging skills but increase in people's awareness to seek maternal care. However no studies are available to figure out consequences of increased people's expectation through JSY and failure of health system to deliver care.

Apart from the health system infrastructure and facilities, professional staff is an important factor in order to make health system quality care giver. Khan et al. (2010) in a formative study on impact of JSY on family health behaviours in rural Uttar Pradesh concluded that introduction of the JSY has helped to increase the rate of institutional deliveries. It has increased delivery load of public institutions from 37 per cent to 63 per cent. But on the other hand study found social distance and low contact existed between the ASHA and pregnant women in terms of caste, class, religion and education. . Quantitative and qualitative data analysis shows that the majorities of ASHAs (74 per cent) belongs to general caste or other backward caste families, and often are relatives of village leaders and as a result hesitate to visit scheduled caste/ scheduled tribe women. In some cases, the perceived hostility towards or non-acceptance of ASHAs by Muslim families also deprives Muslim families from receiving advice from the ASHA.

Both public and private health sector in India are facing many challenges to meet increasing demand of various types of human resources. Nandan et al. (2012) argues that achievement in health outcome such as MMR and IMR are directly related to density of human resource in health sector. Despite of huge investment through NRHM to deploy new staff, many low performing states are facing shortage of human resource for health.

Rao (2010) conducted a qualitative study of medical students and in-service medical professionals of Uttarakhand and Andhra Pradesh to record their attributes toward rural service in India. Study reveals that both kinds of respondents strongly hesitate to work in rural area because of low infrastructural facilities in health centre, lack of basic needs such as transport, water, electricity, and education in rural areas. Study reveals that only salary package cannot retain professionals in rural area and attention needs to be paid to both salary and non-salary incentives for rural recruitment and retention.

In a similar study on in-service peripheral health worker Rajaretnam et al. (2005) highlighted multitudes of problems faced by peripheral health workers. Apart from personal problems peripheral health workers of Karnataka highlighted several organizational and community level problems. ANM and LHVs highlighted lack of transportation in villages, lack of basic facilities and minimum required furniture and instruments in ANM Centre affects in delivering quality service to villagers. They appreciated IEC system of Pulse Polio campaign and suggested to replicate that in other programmes as well. Study also reveals that due to lack of education among scheduled tribes and schedule castes, there is community resistance for ANC and immunization.

Contrary to an emphasis on trained and professional maternal care giver under JSY, Sadgopal, (2009) highlighted several lacunas in health governance and strengths and richness of knowledge and experience of traditional birth attendants. In remote areas dais (TBA) are deterred from attending births with no alternative provided. The JSY scheme for institutional delivery lacks adequate PHC and referral infrastructure. In rural remote areas inexperienced doctors of PHCs act as superiors over elderly experienced dais. Article highlights valuable practices of Dais in order to carter effective maternal health needs of pregnant mother such as squatting and movement during labour, continuous caregiver support during labour, perineal massage and support during labour, delay in cord-cutting, etc. All these common practices of Dais are found medically correct practices. In the end she argues that there is need of incorporating traditional knowledge in health governance to enhance richness of health system in India.

All of these studies are to know that JSY during the period of NRHM implementation, that is, from 2005 to 2012 has helped in increasing the case load for institutional deliveries. Contrary to this NRHM fail to upgrade health system in order to effectively cater to increased need of the pregnant mother. It is evident from the studies that there is shortage of health professionals in rural area because of many reasons. However studies do not link health facilities, service providers and utilization patterns of different maternal care. JSY has emphasis on intuitional care during entire pregnancy period to ensure safe motherhood. So the linkage between health system availability, physical accessibility and service providers needs to be understood in relation to the utilization pattern of different components of maternal care such as ANC, delivery care and PNC.

2.3 Accessibility of Health System and Quality of Care

Janani Suraksha Yojana (JSY) is not only limited to intuitional deliveries rather it provides quality minimum maternal care during antenatal, natal, and post natal period. Utilization of health services at every level can reduce risk of mothers during their pregnancy. Gupta et al. (2010) focused on quantity and quality of ANC coverage among beneficiaries of JSY in a tertiary care hospital of Madhya Pradesh. Study concludes that antenatal checkups are still not available to or utilized by a large number of beneficiaries even after implementation of JSY. Study further concludes that peripheral health workers should improve ANC with special emphasis on the basic recommended investigation which is found mostly neglected. Study shows that only 16 per cent women were investigated for blood pressure, haemoglobin, urine test and weight record during prenatal care period.

Deshpande (2011), using the survey data on Rapid Appraisal of NRHM in Koppal district of Karnataka analyzed to find out whether JSY scheme is helping to reduce maternal and infant mortality. Survey analysis revealed that a majority of women are still unable to avail benefits of JSY. Report clearly concluded that JSY scheme is not successfully reaching the goal of reducing maternal and infant mortality in the district. The study reveals that only 40 per cent of deliveries among the JSY beneficiaries were institutional, the remaining were at home. It found that lack of awareness and motivation from peripheral workers is responsible for such a low coverage. From the area of study only two-third of eligible JSY beneficiaries were enrolled for the scheme. And out of enrolled women only 25 per cent of pregnant women had enrolled during the first trimester. A large portion of women who opted for home delivery think that it is convenient at home followed by un-affordable cost of hospital as reason for opting home delivery.

Despite the increased access that JSY offers, its a question still why do women continue to opt delivery at home; the reasons for home delivery appear to cover three areas of behavioral, financial and institutional dimensions. Kaulagekar-Nagarkar, (2012) concluded his study about influencing factors for place of delivery among slum dwellers of Pimpri-Chinchwad of Maharashtra that there is strong linkage between use of antenatal care and place of delivery. The study found that mostly respondents from scheduled caste and scheduled tribe groups prefer home delivery. It is evident from the study that these groups are poorest slum dwellers and the average cost of delivery services in public institution was rupees six hundred while in private was rupees five thousand.

Even though studies show low coverage of JSY services, but the literature highlighted relative increase in institutional deliveries (Planning Commission 2011, Khan 2010, DRS 2009). Gupta et al. (2012) conducted an observational study in a tertiary level health institution of Madhya Pradesh to understand the impact of JSY on institutional delivery rate, maternal mortality and morbidity. The study found an increase of 42.6 per cent in institutional deliveries after implementation of JSY. The scheme has helped rural poor women to overcome their financial barriers and motivated them to come for institutional delivery. Many JSY respondents were availing health system facilities for the first time. The authors concluded that the motivators under this scheme were able to identify the women at high risk of maternal care and referred them timely to higher level service centres. The study also noted anemia as the most common underlying cause of maternal death.

The fact of increased institutional delivery is also supported by Gaur, et al. (2012) based on a desk research using data from health department of Gwalior district in Madhya Pradesh. The study found that there is sharp increase in institutional deliveries from 48.44 per cent in 2003-04 to 73 per cent in 2007-08. Regarding ante natal care services to pregnant women, the study found no any significant increase in its utilization. Only 32 per cent of women are accessing three or more ante natal care services.

Institutional delivery is not sufficient to achieve status of safe motherhood. Lahariya (2009) in his article describes JSY as a desired and people centric health program in the country that evolved from previous experiences and carrying best practices from the past. He found significant impact of JSY on institutional deliveries. He also suggests expanding the cash incentive even for prenatal care to enhance maternal health outcome of the nation. The article comprehensively highlighted policy issues related to JSY. He emphasised on institutional deliveries and not significantly providing facilities for ante natal and post natal care.

Studies in different parts of India suggest measures to increase full maternal care to pregnant women. Development and Research Services (DRS) (2009) in a UNFPA sponsored research investigated implementation status of Janani Suraksha Yojana in five low performing states of India concludes that in all surveyed states JSY is a popular scheme and it has increased institutional deliveries. But to attain desirable goal of 80 per cent institutional deliveries, there is a need to create more capacity in the health system. The study identified various gaps in effective implementation of JSY. It recommends focusing on enhancing quality of care and community mobilization for better results. Study documented a sharp increase in institutional deliveries. The other determinants of utilization of maternal care is state specific and based on socio-economic category. It clearly reveals that vulnerable groups such as Dalit, Adivasis, and Minorities are not yet able to access health facilities as good as their other counterparts are receiving.

Delivery of effective health services such as ANC, institutional delivery and PNC in Uttarakhand is highly difficult due to hilly and forest covered geographical conditions. Poor transport connectivity and lack of institutional arrangements in hilly villages makes difficult to provide effective health services to common people. Constella Futures (2012), implemented an operational research project in Public Private Partnership mode in selected hilly district of Uttarakhand to strengthen mechanism and capacity of ASHAs in order to make people access health service. Using local resources, knowledge, placing effective monitoring system and applying innovation in capacity development of ASHAs project at the end of two years resulted in tremendous growth in utilization of maternal and child health services. Institutional delivery increased from 27 per cent to 58 per cent. Percentage of women received minimum three ANC rose from 30 to 46 per cent and early registration of pregnant women increased from 35 per cent to 65 per cent.

Janani Suraksha Yojana provides inclusiveness for weaker and poor mothers of India. It has integrated cash assistance with delivery and post delivery care. Studies on JSY also highlighted the fact that cash incentives have increased institutional delivery among socially disadvantaged and poor people, and that the antenatal care and postnatal care among these groups remain poor. Nevertheless, this chapter describes the quality of maternal health care from different parts of India. Hence this chapter shows that utilization of antenatal and post natal care is still very low among beneficiaries of JSY.

Chapter - 3

Health Status Profile of Uttarakhand

Various studies on maternal health have already established the fact that utilization of health care and maternal wellbeing is affected by a number of socio-economic and demographic variables. These along with different comprehensive statistics indicate that the programme has not ensured safe motherhood. Present chapter is an attempt to look into this particular knowledge gap regarding Janani Suraksha Yojana in Uttarakhand.

Health outcomes of India are evident that economically poor and socially disadvantaged groups such as Schedule caste and schedule tribes who have poor access to health system. More than 60 per cent women from SCs don't have access to safe delivery and only 20 per cent economically poor women can avail institutions for safe delivery (NFHS-III). According to a study of UNICEF 80 per cent of maternal death occurs in poor families. Sixty one per cent of women who died were from Dalit and Adivasis (Kumar 2010). Caste and poverty are well recognized factors in maternal health programmes and policies of India (Nayar 2011). Janani Suraksha Yojana brings the poor, excluded and marginalized women closer to the health services system through a facilitating and participatory approach. A study by Digambar et al. (2011) reveals that full ANC is substantially higher for those who belong to other caste (23 per cent) compared to SC/ST women (12 per cent). Delivery care utilization is also less among SC/ST women (28 per cent) as compared to women belong to other castes (43 per cent). Apart from caste, rural and urban settings too contribute to differences in maternal health utilization. Full ANC care is almost three times higher among women from urban area (38 per cent) compare to rural women (13 per cent). Post natal care is also very low among women from SC/ST category and rural area. Only 26 per cent women from SC/ST caste have accessed post natal care. Study concludes that though women use antenatal care, many of them do not get professional care during delivery. The major obstacles of the institutional delivery are traditional attitudes and cultural beliefs. Economic condition of family affects their accessibility to health system. NSHRC (2011) in an evaluation of Janani Suraksha Yojana in different states including Uttarakhand found that one third of deliveries take place at home. The pregnant women are not able to access institutions on account of not being able to afford transport costs, poor service quality and high costs in institutions and cultural preferences. The report also indicated that out-of-pocket payments were high, amounting to Rs. 1028, and including transport, to about ₹ 1400 to ₹ 1600. The main out-of-pocket expenditures in institutional delivery are on drugs, but there were significant expenses on fees and on surgery.

Table 3.1: Comparative Profile of Demographic, Socio-Economic and Health Indicators of Uttarakhand

Pointers	*Uttarakhand*	*India*
Total Population (In Crore) *	1.01	121.01
Decadal Growth (%) *	19.17	17.64
Crude Birth Rate **	18.9	21.8
Crude Death Rate **	6.2	7.1
Infant Mortality Rate **	36	44
Maternal Mortality Rate ***	359	212
Total Fertility Rate**	NA	2.4
Sex Ratio *	963	940
Child Sex Ratio *	886	914
Schedule Caste population (In Crore) *	0.15	16.67
Schedule Tribe population (in crore) *	0.02	8.43
Total Literacy Rate (%) *	79.63	74.04
Male Literacy Rate (%) *	88.33	82.14
Female Literacy Rate (%) *	70.70	65.46

Source: *Census 2011**; Sample Registration System 2011**
Sample Registration System 2007-09***

As per Sample Registration System (2007-2009) the Infant Mortality Rate (IMR) is 38 and Maternal Mortality Ratio (MMR) is 359, which are higher than the national average. The female-male sex ratio in the state is 963 (as compared to 940 for India as a whole). The **Table 3.1** above provides data of main health and demographic indicators comparative to national figures.

3.1 Public Health Institutions and Professionals

National Rural Health Mission (2005-2012), was formally launched in Uttarakhand on 27th of October 2005. The focus of mission in Uttarakhand was to achieve clearly defined goals by strengthening primary health care through grass root level public health interventions based on community ownership. Along with many other targets, the state had the target to reduce maternal mortality rate upto 100, decrease infant mortality rate upto 38 and increase institutional delivery up to 80 per cent. Achieving different targets of NRHM, the state has planned to bring reform in public health sector especially by increasing number of health professionals at different capacities in different institutions.

Table 3.2: Health Professionals in Public Health Institutions

Key Health Professionals	*Sectioned*	*Vacant*
ANM at Sub-Centre	2077	00
Doctor at PHC	299	65
Gynaecologists at CHC	55	35
Paediatricians at CHC	45	18
Surgeon at CHC	55	38
Total specialists at CHC (Surgeon, OB&GY, Physician & Paediatrician)	210	132

Source: RHS, 2011.

Rural Health Statistics (2011) compiled by Statistics Division of Ministry of Health and Family Welfare (GoI) recorded an increase in health professionals in Uttarakhand with different capacity in different public health institutions. There is also an increase in number of public health institutions during NRHM period. But the same report also reveals that state has not made progress in ensuring sufficient number of health professionals to ensure access of rural population in Uttarakhand (**Table 3.2**). The data finds that there are 32 Sub-Centres where there is no ANM positioned, around 30 per cent of Primary Health Centers (PHCs) have no doctors. Lab technicians are important paramedical staff in providing quality maternal care, but in this state around 54 per cent of PHCs do not have any lab technicians.

Uttarakhand is one among high focus states of NRHM and hence had opportunity to avail maximum facilities provided by this mission. It is the only hill state among eight EAG (Empowered Action Group) states of India. Though it is a small state in India there exists a wide range of disparities within different parts of this state. Infant mortality rate ranges from 19 in Rudraprayag district to 72 in Haridwar district. Similarly Child mortality ranges from 24 in Pithoragarh district to 94 in Haridwar.

Table 3.3: Progress in Maternal and Child Health

Indicator	*Goal for 2012 (NRHM)*	*Pre-NRHM status of Health Indicators*	*Current Status of Health Indicator*
Infant Mortality Rate	30	42 (MoHFW, 2011)	43 (AHS, 2011)
Complete Immunization of children	100%	62.99% (NFHS-III)	75.8% (CES, 2009)
Maternal Mortality Ratio	100	440 (MoHFW,2011) combined with Uttar Pradesh	188 (AHS, 2011)
Institutional Delivery	80%	36% (NFHS-III)	53.5 (CES, 2009)

The comparison of statistics from different sources shows that NRHM goals appear very distant even after completion of NRHM phase. After Jharkhand, Uttarakhand has shown the least progress in increasing institutional delivery in rural areas from 2005 to 2009 (CES, 2009). During this period Uttarakhand managed to increase institutional delivery by 23 per cent. It is an opportunity through this study to investigate the factors behind low maternal health outcome in the sample districts even after implementation of Janani Suraksha Yojana under NRHM for more than seven years. And thus find out factors that hinder Janani Suraksha Yojana (JSY) in achieving goal of safe motherhood in the state of Uttarakhand (**Table 3.3**).

With a large number of public health institutions in rural areas from Sub-Centres at the most peripheral level to the district hospitals at the district level, India has made noteworthy achievements in improvement of health indicators over the last few decades. Initiation of the National Rural Health Mission in 2005 further armoured its commitment to improve health indicators and attain the universal Millennium Development Goals.

Chapter - 4

Access and Utilization of Janani Suraksha Yojana in Uttarakhand

This chapter deals with the assessment of accessibility and utilisation of Janani Suraksha Yojana at three levels, namely, ante-natal care, delivery, and post-natal care from two sample districts of Uttarakhand; Haridwar, a district in the plains and Almora, located in the hills. The primary respondents were women who had delivered in the one year preceding the interview. This field-level research study is complemented with in-depth case studies of respondents. Moreover, analysis is also done with regard to the kind of institutional support received from ASHA, ANM and other service providers at various levels. An attempt is also made to understand the level of awareness about JSY among the respondents, the interplay of background variables such as caste category, geographical location such as hill / plain and rural / urban, income, religion etc. This provides available evidence about the implementation of the JSY and its impact on women's access and utilisation to maternal health services after the introduction of the JSY and to investigate gaps if any in promoting safe delivery, the stated objective of JSY. The analysis also provides better understanding of the benefits claimed under JSY and problems encountered in utilising the medical services and benefits.

This field-level research study presents findings from a survey of in-depth case studies of women who had experienced maternal delivery in the one year preceding the interview as well as other stakeholders.This serves available evidence about the implementation of the JSY and its impact on women's access and utilisation to maternal health services after the introduction of the JSY to investigate maternal health care practices. In the present study, two districts have been selected from the state of Uttarakhand, these are Haridwar, representing the Plains; and Almora, representing the Hills. This chapter deals with the assessment of access and utilisation of Janani Suraksha Yojana, wherein the beneficiary women were interviewed to understand their background, their awareness about JSY, and the kind of institutional support received from ASHA, ANM and other service providers at various levels. The study also attempts to understand the experience of claiming benefits under JSY and problems encountered in utilising the medical services and benefits.

4.1 Characteristics of Respondents' Households

This section provides information about the selected respondent (women) pertaining to their households who participated in the study as beneficiaries or partial beneficiaries of Janani Suraksha Yojana (JSY). These selected characteristics include their–geographical location, social categories, religion, educational status, housing type, family type, income, and occupation.

Table 4.1a: Location-Wise Respondent Households in Uttarakhand

	Plains (Haridwar)			*Hills (Almora)*			*Both*		
	Rural	*Urban*	*Total*	*Rural*	*Urban*	*Total*	*Rural*	*Urban*	*Total*
Percentage	68.1	31.9	210	90.3	9.7	103	75.4	24.6	313
Number	143	67		93	10		236	77	

In terms of location, overall, a set of 313 households were selected, which comprised of 210 (67 per cent) households from Plains (Haridwar) and 103 (33 per cent) households from Hills (Almora). In terms of residence, out of these 313 households, 236 (75 per cent),were from rural area (involving highest proportion of 60.6 per cent from Haridwar district and a lowest proportion of 39.4 per cent from Almora district), and 77 (25 per cent) were from urban area (involving a higher proportion of 87 per cent from Haridwar district and a lower proportion of 13 per cent from Almora district) **(Table 4.1a)**.

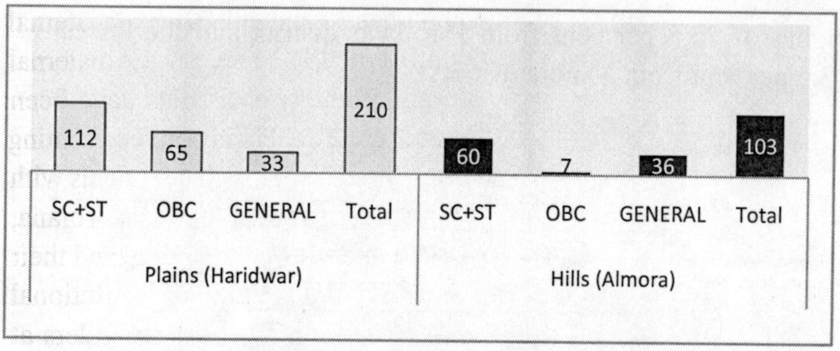

Figure 4.1a: Caste Categorisation of Respondent Mothers

In terms of social groups, overall a maximum of 172 (55 per cent) belonged to SC-ST (scheduled caste cum scheduled tribe) group; 72 (23 per cent) belonged to OBC (other backward caste) group; and a minimum of 69 (22 per cent) belonged to General group. Further, out of these 172 households belonging to SC-ST group, 65.1 per cent were from Haridwar district and 34.9 per cent were from Almora district. Out of 72 households belonging to OBC group 90.3 per cent were from Haridwar district and 9.7 per cent were from Almora district). Out of 69 households belonging to General group, 47.8 per cent were from Haridwar district and 52.2 per cent were from Almora district.

Figure 4.1a illustrates the social groups of interviewed respondents from both districts of Haridwar and Almora . Out of an overall 210 selected respondents from Haridwar district, a higher proportion of 112 (53.3 per cent) belonged to SC-ST group, 65 (31 per cent) belonged to OBC group and 33 (15.7 per cent) belonged to General group. Whereas out of an overall 103 selected respondents from Almora district, a higher proportion of 60 (58.3 per cent) belonged to SC-ST group, 7 (6.8 per cent) belonged to OBC group and 36 (35 per cent) belonged to General group.

In terms of religion, 296 (95 per cent) were from Hindu religion, (involving a higher proportion of 66.6 per cent from Haridwar district and a lower proportion of 33.4 per cent from Almora district) and 17 (5 per cent) were from Muslim and Sikh religions (involving a higher of 76.5 per cent from Haridwar district and the lowest of 23.5 per cent from Almora district).

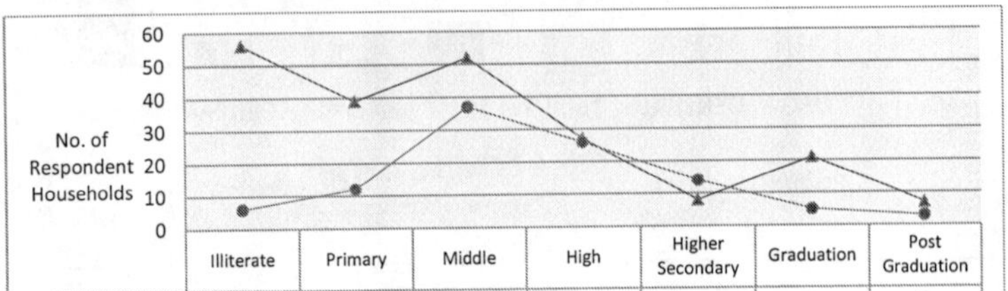

	Illiterate	Primary	Middle	High	Higher Secondary	Graduation	Post Graduation
Haridwar	56	39	52	27	8	21	7
Almora	6	12	37	26	14	5	3

Figure 4.1b: Educational Status of Respondent Mothers

In terms of education, 62 (20 per cent) respondents were found illiterates (maximum of 90.3 per cent from Haridwar district and minimum of 9.7 per cent from Almora district); 17 per cent were from Primary education level (maximum of 76.5 per cent from Haridwar district and 23.5 per cent from Almora district); 28 per cent are educated up to middle school level (maximum of 58.4 per cent from Haridwar district and Minimum of 41.6 per cent from Almora district); 17 per cent are educated up to High school level (maximum of 50.9 per cent from Haridwar district and minimum of 41.6 per cent from Almora district); 17 per cent are educated up to Higher Secondary level (minimum of 36.4 per cent from Haridwar district and maximum of 63.6 per cent from Almora district); 7 per cent are educated up to Graduation level (maximum of 80.8 per cent from Haridwar district and 19.2 per cent from Almora district); and just 3 per cent are educated up to the level of Post Graduation (maximum of 70 per cent from Haridwar district and minimum of 30 per cent from Almora district). Educational differentials, as reflected in the table, the point of discussion is that the reach of the Janani Suraksha Yojana augmented among those women with no schooling or illiterate to among those women who have completed years of schooling, and declined thereafter among those women who still have completed more years of education **(Figure 4.1b)**.

In terms of Housing type, 11 per cent respondent (women) belonged to Kachcha house type (maximum of 63.6 per cent were from Haridwar district and minimum of 36.4 per cent were from Almora District); 33 per cent respondent (women) belonged to Semi-Kachcha house type (maximum of 57.8 per cent were from Haridwar district and minimum of 42.2 per cent were from Almora District); and 56 per cent respondent women living in Pucca house type (maximum of 73 per cent were from Haridwar district and minimum of 27 per cent were from Almora District).

In terms of Family type, an overall 67 per cent respondent (women) belong to Joint family type (maximum of 64.1 per cent were from Haridwar district and minimum of 35.9 per cent were from Almora District); and 33 per cent respondent (women) belonged to Nuclear family type (maximum of 73.1 per cent were from Haridwar district and minimum of 26.9 per cent were from Almora District).

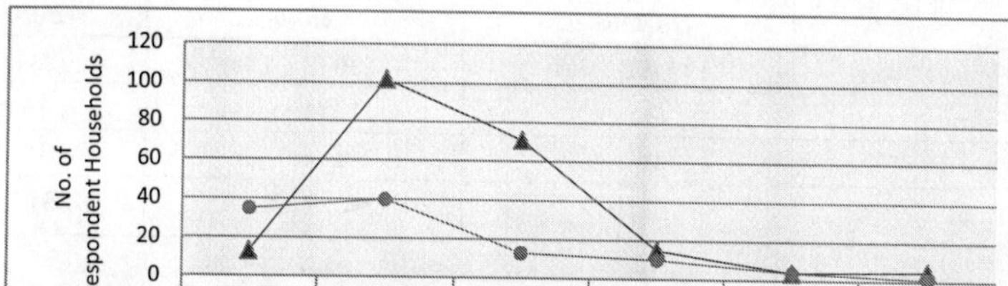

	Upto Rs 25000	Rs.25001 - 50000	Rs.50001 - 75000	Rs.75001 - 100000	Rs.100001 - 150000	Above Rs.150000
Haridwar	13	102	71	15	4	5
Almora	35	40	13	10	4	1

Figure 4.1c: Household Income of Respondent Mothers

In terms of Income status, 15 per cent sample Households taken as sample selected for this study, belonged to an income group of up to ₹ 25000/= per year (maximum of 72.9 per cent were from Almora district and minimum of 27.1 per cent were from Haridwar District); 45 per cent belonged to an annual income group of 25001- ₹ 50000 (maximum of 71.8 per cent were from Haridwar district and minimum of 28.2 per cent were from Almora District); 27 per cent study households belonged to an annual income group of ₹ 50001-75000 (maximum of 84.5 per cent were from Haridwar district and minimum of 15.5 per cent were from Almora District); 8 per cent interviewed households belonged to an annual income group of ₹ 75001-₹ 100000 (maximum of 60 per cent were from Haridwar district and minimum of 40 per cent were from Almora District); just 3 per cent belonged to an income group of ₹ 100001-150000 per year (an equal proportion of 50 per cent were each from Haridwar district as well as Almora district);and merely 2 per cent households belonged to an annual income of more than ₹ 150000 (maximum of 83.3 per cent were from Haridwar district and 16.7 per cent were from Almora District). With reference to economic differentials, observations suggest that not considering of their place of residence, or even geographical location in general, those women belonging to households of poor background were less possibly than others to have obtained the benefits under Janani Suraksha Yojana **(Figure 4.1c)**.

Table 4.1b: Occupational Status of Respondent Mothers

	Haridwar	*Almora*	*Both*
Home Maker	195 (92.8 %)	86 (83.4 %)	281
Farming	2 (1.0 %)	13 (12.6 %)	15
Others	13 (6.2 %)	4 (4.0 %)	17
Total	**210**	**103**	**313**

In terms of occupational profile, an overall 90 per cent sample respondents were Homemakers (maximum of 69.4 per cent were from Haridwar district and minimum of 30.6 per cent were from Almora District); an equal of 5 per cent each belonged to Farming category (minimum of 13.3 per cent were from Haridwar district and 86.7 per cent were from Almora District), other categories (maximum of 76.5 per cent were from Haridwar district and minimum of 23.5 per cent were from Almora District) **(Table 4.1b)**.

In terms of occupational profile, an overall 90 per cent sample respondents were Homemakers (maximum of 69.4 per cent were from Haridwar district and minimum of 30.6 per cent were from Almora District); an equal of 5 per cent each belonged to Farming category (minimum of 13.3 per cent were from Haridwar district and 86.7 per cent were from Almora District), others category (maximum of 76.5 per cent were from Haridwar district and minimum of 23.5 per cent were from Almora District).

4.2 Practices of Health Care by Respondent Women and Extent of JSY Use

The following sections present experiences of respondent women in accessing and utilising the JSY and availing its benefits in hilly (Almora) and in plain (Haridwar) geographical locations of Uttarakhand. In particular, it deals with the reach of the JSY, the extent to which JSY beneficiaries have received its benefits, reasons for not availing of JSY benefits among partial beneficiaries or non-beneficiaries, and finally, their perceptions about the JSY. This also focuses on findings that pertain to the contributions of the JSY to women's utilisation of maternal health services and taking on of practices within their reach. In particular, it investigates the effects of the JSY on the services received by these women during the antenatal period, at delivery time and during the postnatal period.

The utilisation of antenatal care services was assessed by four indicators, namely, whether women had registered her pregnancy in her first trimester under Janani Suraksha Yojana, received an antenatal check-up during the first trimester, whether they had received three or more antenatal check-ups, whether they had received two or more doses of tetanus toxoid injection, and whether they had received or purchased iron and folic acid (IFA) supplements. The utilisation of delivery care services was assessed by indicators, namely, whether the pregnant women went for institutional delivery, whether ASHA escorted to institution for delivery, whether cash incentive was received for institutional delivery, whether they received referral transport from institution in case of pregnancy complications, and whether free transport facility to drop at home was offered after delivery was received. The utilisation of postnatal care services was assessed by indicators, namely, whether the pregnant women stayed in institution for more than 48 hours after delivery, whether they ever gone for PNC checkups to any institution within 42 days after the delivery, and whether ever counselled by ASHA/ANM for womens' own health and child care.

Table 4.2: Sources of Maternal Health Care Services

	Plains (Haridwar)				Hills (Almora)			
	SC+ST	*OBC*	*General*	*Total*	*SC+ST*	*OBC*	*General*	*Total*
Largely in JSY/Govt. Hospital	60	25	6	**91**	48	6	28	**82**
	53.6%	38.5%	18.2%	**43.3%**	80.0%	85.7%	77.8%	**79.6%**
Home (Traditional)		1	1	**2**	2		1	**3**
		1.5%	3.0%	**1.0%**	3.3%	-	2.8%	**2.9%**
Started with JSY but ended in Home	17	7		**24**	9		6	**15**
	15.2%	10.8%	-	**11.4%**	15.0%	-	16.7%	**14.6%**
Started with JSY but ended in Private	11	8	3	**22**	1	1	1	**3**
	9.8%	12.3%	9.1%	**10.5%**	1.7%	14.3%	2.8%	**2.9%**
Combination of JSY, Home, Private	1	1	1	**3**				
	.9%	1.5%	3.0%	**1.4%**	-	-	-	-
Private	23	23	22	**68**				
	20.5%	35.4%	66.7%	**32.4%**	-	-	-	-
Total	112	65	33	**210**	60	7	36	**103**
	100.0%	100.0%	100.0%	**100.0%**	100.0%	100.0%	100.0%	**100.0%**

An analysis of the type of health service utilization of selected respondent women in Uttarakhand revealed that out of 313 respondents a higher proportion of, 173 (55.3 per cent) had largely accessed governmental maternal health care sources or services of Janine Suraksha Yojana (JSY) (involving minimum of 43.3 per cent in Haridwar district and maximum of 79.6 per cent in Almora district); followed by 22 per cent (68) respondents who availed the services only from Private sector in Haridwar district; 12.5 per cent (39) were those respondents who started with JSY maternal health services but ended with delivery at home (involving minimum of 11.4 per cent in Haridwar district and maximum of 14.6 per cent in Almora district); 8 per cent (25) were those respondents who started availing JSY maternal health services but ended with delivery in Private sector health institutions (involving maximum of 10.5 per cent in Haridwar district and minimum of 2.9 per cent in Almora district); 1.6 per cent (5) were those respondents who had undergone their deliveries at home using traditional delivery system (involving minimum of 1 per cent in Haridwar district and 2.9 per cent in Almora district); and 1 per cent (3) were those respondents who had availed maternal health services from a mixture of JSY, home-based and Private sector services in Haridwar district (**Table 4.2**).

Proportionally, JSY utilization was found to be higher in Almora district (97.1 per cent) than in Haridwar district (66.6 per cent), either exclusively or in combination with ending up with home delivery or delivery at private institution. In terms of social category, all the women including 7 OBCs, 35 General castes and 58 SC-STs in Almora district; and 79.5 per cent SC-STs, 63.1 per cent OBCs in Haridwar district were users of JSY. There were three (2.9 per cent) JSY users one each from SC-ST, OBC, and General caste in Almora district who ended with delivery in private institution, but there was no exclusive case of private institution. Whereas, in Haridwar district 44.3 per cent were users of private institution either in combination with JSY or exclusively availed services of private institution.

While categorizing the interviewed respondents in terms of the extent of use of health services under Janani Suraksha Yojana (JSY) it was noted that in the plain areas (Haridwar district) out of 210

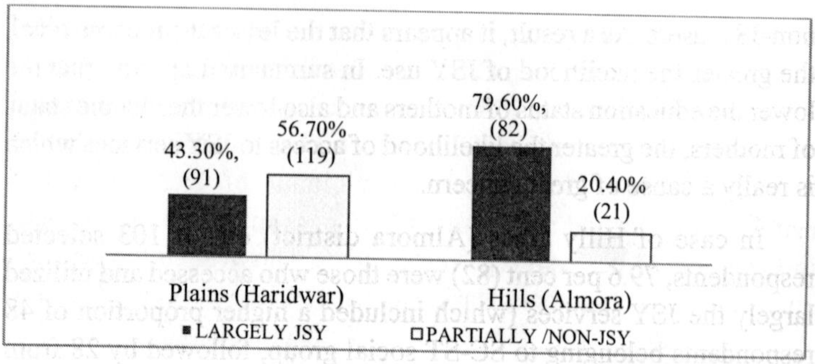

Figure 4.2a: Extent of JSY Use in Haridwar and Almora.

selected respondents 43.3 per cent (91) were those who accessed and utilized the JSY services (which included a highest proportion of 60 respondents belonging to SC-ST social group, followed by 25 from OBC social group and just 6 from General category); and 56.70 per cent (119) were those respondents who either used JSY services partially or did not use at all.

Further exploration across various education categories it was noted that overall out of 173 respondents, nearly 61 mothers were found completed education upto primary school level, 99 mothers of middle to higher secondary level were observed to access largely the JSY services; while on the contrary 52 respondents were found completed education upto primary level, 65 respondents whose education level was between middle to higher secondary level were the partial or non-JSY users. And a number of just 13 mothers with graduation and above were large users of JSY services, while 23 mothers with graduation and above education were partial or non-JSY users. Thus, it appears that the lesser the educational level, the greater the likelihood of JSY use. In the same manner, overall, out of 173 respondents, 169 women mothers whose household income was upto ₹ 1 Lac per year were reported to access JSY to a large extent; while on the contrary 130 respondents, whose household income was upto ₹ 1 Lac per year were the partial or non-JSY users. On the other hand, just 4 women whose household income with above ₹ 1 Lac per year were using JSY services to a large extent and there were 10 women whose household income above ₹ 1 Lac per year were the partial or non-JSY users. As a result, it appears that the lesser the income level, the greater the likelihood of JSY use. In summary it appears that the lower the education status of mothers and also lower the income status of mothers, the greater the likelihood of access to JSY services which is really a cause of great concern.

In case of Hilly areas (Almora district) out of 103 selected respondents, 79.6 per cent (82) were those who accessed and utilized largely the JSY services (which included a higher proportion of 48 respondents belonging to SC-ST social group, followed by 28 from General category and 6 from OBC social group); and 20.4 per cent (21) were those respondents who either used JSY services partially or did not use at all. Thus, it can be stated that on an overall basis, out of 313 interviewed respondents 55.2 per cent (173) were largely the JSY services users; it was only in case of Haridwar district that the percentage of respondents were higher in case of partial JSY use or non-use of JSY maternal health services (**Figure 4.2a; Figure 4.2b**).

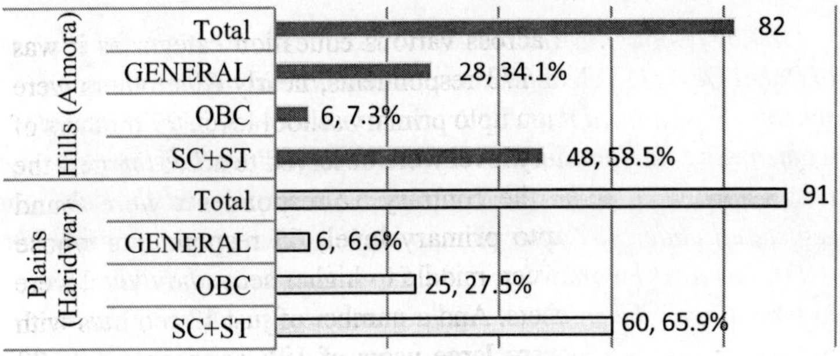

Figure 4.2b: Extent of JSY Use on the Basis of Social Groups.

Thus, in both the two geographical locations the highest proportion of JSY maternal health services' users belonged to SC-ST category in comparison to OBC and General Caste categories.

Case 4.1: Government Health Institutions Not Conducive So Preference of Private Institutions for Delivery

Roshni Devi, 23 Years, wife of Hukum Singh; Saini OBC; Village Chandrapuri Bangar; Block Khanpur; District Haridwar

According to Roshni Devi, the facilities available in the government hospitals are not good. Many a times, doctors are not available. These hospitals are not clean. And the behaviour of the staff towards patients is not up to the mark. In case a caretaker from the family needs to stay with the patient at night, there are no arrangements for the same. Also the family members as caretakers are not treated well. Often no arrangements are made available at these hospitals for the patients even to sit properly. On the hot sunny days patients are made to stand in a queue under the sun in the heat. As the facilities are not good she went to a private hospital for her treatment. Roshni Devi and her family opined that private hospitals are much better in terms of providing treatment as compared to the government hospital.

Case 4.2: Benefitted by JSY Due to Family Support, No Support Received from ANM and ASHA

Rakhi Devi, 23 Years, wife of Rishipal; OBC; Village Ranimajra; Post Shahapur Sheetlakheda; Block Bhadarabad; District Haridwar

While conducting the survey on JSY the team reached the house of Rakhi Devi (JSY Beneficiary) and enquired about her views on the scheme. She claimed that JSY is a very important scheme initiated for women. She has obtained benefits out of it since the time she got pregnant and after her delivery too. She explained that she got registered under JSY after three months of her pregnancy with the ANM. The ASHA worker has not informed anybody about the Scheme in the village. She said that she has taken care of herself during the pregnancy and her family also supported in this endeavour. Neither the ANM nor the ASHA worker has informed about the care, vaccination, diet, medicine etc to be taken during pregnancy. The iron tablets were not provided to her by the government facilities rather she had to buy these from the market. She has not received any help from the ASHA worker and she has gone without any aid except that from her husband to get her routine medical checkups done. When her labour pains started, her husband took her to the district government hospital. According to her, the hospital nurses and staff took her care adequately. She found that doctor's attitude and behaviour was good. The hospital was clean and she never had any trouble during her stay at the hospital. Her son was born on June 17, 2012 and he was healthy. She went again to the hospital one week after her release and received the cheque for ₹ 1400/ under the incentive scheme. She felt that the Scheme is quiet useful and every women should receive benefit under such Scheme.

4.3: Problems Faced by Partial-Users or Non-Users of Janani Suraksha Yojana

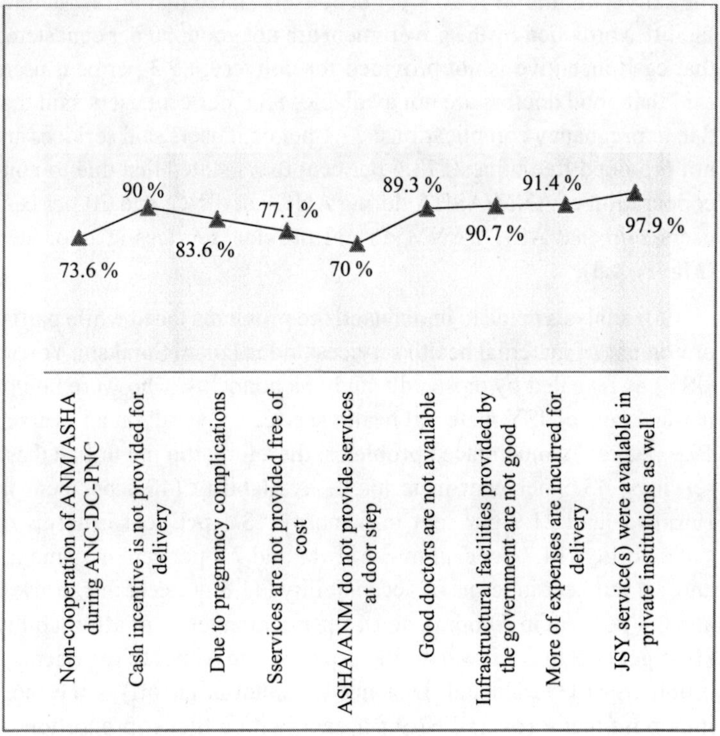

Figure 4.3: Reasons Behind Non-JSY/Partial JSY Service Use (N = 140)

The main reasons behind "partial use" of JSY maternal health services in Uttarakhand as revealed by those 140 interviewed respondents, who were non or partial users of JSY services, included– non-cooperation of ANM/ASHA during antenatal care, delivery care, postnatal care services; cash incentive is not provided for delivery;

due to pregnancy complications, services are not provided free of cost; ASHA/ANM do not provide services at door step; good doctors are not available; infrastructural facilities provided by the government are not good; more of expenses are incurred for delivery; JSY service(s) were available in private institutions as well; and others. A higher proportion of 97.9 per cent users stated that service(s) that are provided under JSY are also available in private institutions as well; followed by 91.4 per cent users who stated that more of expenses are incurred for delivery under JSY; 90.7 per cent users stated that infrastructural facilities provided by the government are not good; 90 per cent stated that cash incentive is not provided for delivery; 89.3 per cent users said that good doctors are not available; 83.6 per cent users said that due to pregnancy complications; 77.1 per cent users said services are not provided free of cost; 73.6 per cent users stated that due to non-cooperation of ANM/ASHA during ANC-DC-PNC; and 70 per cent users said that ASHA/ANM do not provide services at door step **(Figure 4.3)**.

An analysis made to understand the problems faced while partial or non use of maternal health services under Janani Suraksha Yojana (JSY) as revealed by those 140 study respondents, who were non or partial users of JSY maternal health services. Overall on an average 19.9 per cent women faced problems, therefore, did not utilize these services, 43.5 per cent in terms of availability (48.5 per cent in Haridwar and 21.9 per cent in Almora), 13.6 per cent in terms of accessibility (14.7 per cent in Haridwar and 7.2 per cent in Almora), and 7.4 per cent in terms of acceptability (11.3 per cent in Haridwar and 6.4 per cent in Almora), and 15 per cent in terms of affordability (16.4 per cent in Haridwar and 14.3 per cent in Almora), experienced problems in Uttarakhand. Distance (hospital is far off) is the most important factor (overall 67.9 per cent, with a higher proportion of 76.2 per cent in Hill district than 66.4 per cent in Plain district); no privacy in hospitals reported by 31.1 per cent respondents in Haridwar; government hospitals don't have competent human resources reported by a higher 47 per cent women respondents in Haridwar than 9.5 per cent in Almora district; feeling of insecurity reported by a higher proportion of 56.3 per cent in Haridwar district than 4.8 per cent in Almora district, and most importantly the factor that government hospitals are unable to handle pregnancy complications as reported by a higher proportion of 46.2 per cent of study respondents in Haridwar district than 14.3 per cent in Almora district (in terms of availability); shyness among those women to share about their pregnancy related issues with others was the most important factor (17.8 per cent) (in terms of acceptability); have experienced that government hospital care is time consuming (with a higher proportion of 30.3 per cent in Haridwar than 14.3 per cent in Almora), and 2.5 per cent respondent women only from Haridwar district stated that they could not afford the cost involved (in terms of affordability) which contributed towards partial-use or non-use of JSY services (**Figure 4.4**).

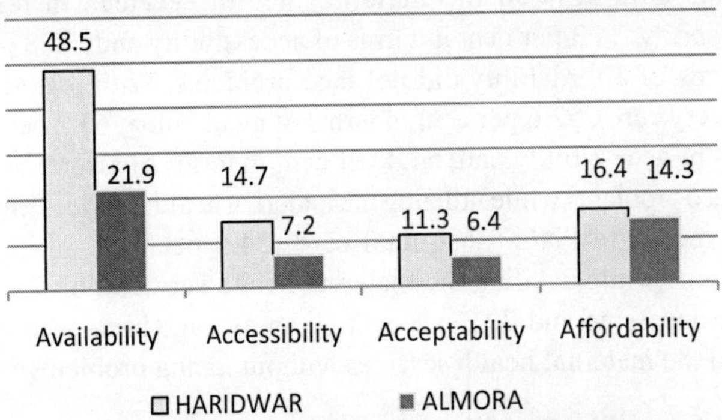

Figure 4.4: Problems Faced While Partial or Non-Utilisation of JSY Services (Percentage Points)

Mother's health replicates in health of babies and pregnancy complications. Dasgupta et al. (2012) in a study conducted about the status of ante natal care of selected post natal mothers in a tertiary care hospital in Calcutta. The study covered women from all economic categories and found that only 36.5 per cent women had registered in the first trimester of pregnancy. The study further found a statistically significant increase in utilization of antenatal care with the increase of educational status and socio-economic status of mothers. Frequency of low birth weight babies was found significantly more among mothers visiting antenatal clinics less than three times as compared to mothers visiting more than three times. Study also found that during the ante natal care counseling received by mothers on diet, hygiene, family planning and breast feeding was very low.

An analysis of the extent of the level of JSY maternal health care received by its beneficiary respondents while accessing and/or utilizing these services, in terms of the availability, accessibility and affordability of these services in Uttarakhand as revealed by those 173 study respondents who were largely the users of JSY maternal health services, overall, it was observed that 46.8 per cent did not face problems in terms of availability, 53.7 per cent in terms of accessibility and 56.8 per cent in terms of affordability. With regard to ANC (ante-natal care), it was noted that 32.9 per cent beneficiary respondents utilized the maternal health services in terms of availability, 34.3 per cent in terms of accessibility and, 35.8 per cent in terms of affordability did not face problems. With regard to DC (delivery care), 52.6 per cent in terms of availability, 63.2 per cent in terms of accessibility and, 64.4 per cent in terms of affordability did not face problems while utilizing the maternal health services. Similarly with regard to PNC (post-natal care) 54.9 per cent did not face problems while availing the maternal health services, 63.7 per cent while accessing and 70.3 per cent on an average basis were able to afford the maternal health services without facing problems.

Case 4.3: All in the Village Deprived of JSY

Village Taya; Block Sult; District Almora

Taya village is 20 kilometers far from Bhikyasen and is located under the territorial division of Sult Block. The path to Taya village from Sult block along the banks of the Ramganga River is about 70 kilometers long. The unrelenting path to this village is composed of 18 kilometers travel, ascent of 176 stairs and further travel of one and a half kilometers through the dense forest area. The village is populated by 1310 individuals. After reaching the village the team met the ASHA worker Tulsi Devi. She expressed her belief that the area she is catering to is geographically widespread and women in the village have to travel 3 kilometers away to a school where the centre is located for immunization purposes. The women from this village need to travel to Bhikyasen, 20 kilometers far from this place or to Ranikhet, 50 kilometers away for child birth and delivery. Occasionally they may travel to Bhatrojkhan which is 50 kilometers away. The CHC centre for this village is 25 kilometers away and located in Majhod, the PHC is located in Sult. The locals told that commonly the deliveries are conducted locally either by the ASHA worker or the midwives in the premises of homes. For all the births taking place in these conditions, none of the mothers has received the sum of Rs. 500. To reach the village the team had to walk our way for 6 hours. None of the women in the area was aware of any such scheme. Not one person in the village has benefitted under the JSY scheme run by the government.

Case 4.4: Sorry State of Affairs in Remote Villages in Hills

Village Nannankota; Block Sult; District Almora

Kaverla is situated 35 kilometers away from Bhikyasen and Nannakota village is further 8 kilometers far from the main road situated at the bank of Ramganga river. The major habitants of this village are people from General category of population or from the Schedule castes. Many of them have migrated to cities. During the JSY study, the elderly from the village informed that no ASHA worker is appointed for this village. ANM never visits for vaccination or immunization. In case there is some difficulty that arises during delivery and child birth then there is no provision available to take her to the hospital. To reach the main road one needs to go through the forest area and then climb the hill. For the purpose of getting delivery done in the hospital, the local people take pregnant women a week or ten days before to their relatives' place. The CHC in Bhikyasen which is equipped to conduct deliveries is 43 kilometers away from this village. However, the Bhikyasen's CHC is also not well equipped to conduct difficult deliveries. In case there is a difficult situation, women are referred to Haldwani or Ranikhet. The locals shared that even to get immunization of pregnant women done they need to travel to Karvela which is 7 kilometers away. The information about JSY programmes reaches only through TV or radio. Otherwise people are not aware of any other schemes and policies initiated by the government.

Case 4.5: Inaccessible Services of ASHA and ANM adds to the Problem

Bhavna Devi, 32 Years; Village Dangikhola; Block Hawalbagh; District Almora

Govindpuri is situated 35 kilometers far from Almora which itself is located 2 kilometers away from Dangikhola. This village falls under the jurisdiction of Block Hawalbagh. The ANM Centre catering to village Dangikhola is situated in Ramna, Govindpuri. The population of Dangikhola village is comprised of mainly people from the General category as well as the Schedule caste (mostly craftsmen), thereby dividing the village into two as per the category of the population inhabiting the area. Agriculture is the major occupation of the people in this village. The educational status of women in this area is quite low as compared to that amongst men. Bhavna Devi is a resident of Dangikhola. Her husband is Chandan Ram who works as a Mason. The couple has one son and Bhavna Devi is expecting again. She has been vaccinated twice for Tetanus. She had to travel in these difficult times to Ranikhet, 20 kilometers away from Dangikhola, for her regular blood pressure checkup, ultrasound and urine test. Bhavna Devi stated that neither the ASHA worker nor the ANM ever visited the village for the purposes of creating awareness regarding the health issues. However, the ASHA worker provides information regarding immunization over phone. Yet, she does not visit when she is called during emergencies like women suffering from labour pains. The ASHA worker visits the ANM Centre only during the days scheduled for immunization. This ANM Centre building is located 3 kilometers from the village and lacks the maternity and child delivery facilities. The ANM for Dangikhola also stays at Almorah.

Case 4.6: Inaccessible ASHA and ANM in Chauna Village, Almora

The village Chauna is divided into two parts. The population of this village is 1000 with 170 families mostly belonging to either General category or Schedule caste (craftsmen) category. There is one ASHA Worker employed in this village. The team contacted the Aanganwadi worker of this village and according to her, neither the

ANM nor the ASHA worker have taken any steps to create awareness about the health issues related to pregnant women, children or the adolescent girls. The ANM Centre for Chauna village is at Daulaghat which is 4 kilometers away from the village and one needs to walk to reach there. According to anganwadi worker, the ANM moves up and down from Almora rather than staying at Daulaghat. There is no facility available for maternity and child delivery at the Centre. Most of the women therefore are compelled to go to Almora or Ranikhet for deliveries. Both these places are around 35 kilometers away from this village.

4.4 Status of Maternal Health Care Utilisation in Uttarakhand

Assessment of actual status of maternal health care in Uttarakhand revealed that out of 173 study respondents who were interviewed it was found that an average of 65.2 per cent women have utilized the benefits under Janani Suraksha Yojana (JSY) effectively. Further, in terms of the three levels of care, 88.9 per cent beneficiary respondents have effectively utilized the services under ANC (ante-natal care) (higher proportion of 94.2 per cent in Almora district and 92.7 per cent in Haridwar district), 54.2 per cent beneficiary respondents effectively utilized the services under Delivery care (a higher proportion of 70.7 per cent in Almora district and 65.1 per cent in Haridwar district); and 52.4 per cent beneficiary respondents effectively utilized the services under PNC (post-natal care) (a higher proportion of 67.4 per cent in Haridwar district and 35.8 per cent in Almora district) (**Figure 4.5).** Haridwar district is higher in terms of its population density as well as poverty level (comprising more of muslim population) in comparison to Almora district. Although high number of institutional deliveries are conducted in government hospitals in Haridwar district in terms of absolute numbers as in Almora district as well, but percentage-wise the figure goes down in Haridwar district due to the relative population density. The attraction towards institutional deliveries in government hospitals in both selected districts is due to the provision of cash incentive. It should be noted that the number of institutional deliveries is more in private hospitals in Haridwar district, whereas the number of institutional deliveries in Almora district is more in government hospitals because the doctors are more easily available in government hospital in Almora district than in Haridwar district. Similarly, access to ante-natal care is more in government hospitals (than in private ones) in Almora district because the beneficiary women can receive the JSY benefits only when registration for JSY is done by them in the ante-natal period of pregnancy, which further includes pregnancy confirmation, TT injection and check-ups. So, additionally, there is no option for beneficiaries in Almora district to access the ante-natal care as well as delivery care other than government hospitals. The post-natal care services does not provide any monetary benefit, and also does not involve any need for vaccination for mothers, and also does not have any incentive money to cover the difficulty as well as cost of transportation in the hilly terrains of Almora district. Further, the post-natal infections is less likely to happen in Almora district due to favourable temperature and climate conditions as compared to that in Haridwar district in plains, which may result in low level of access to post-natal care.

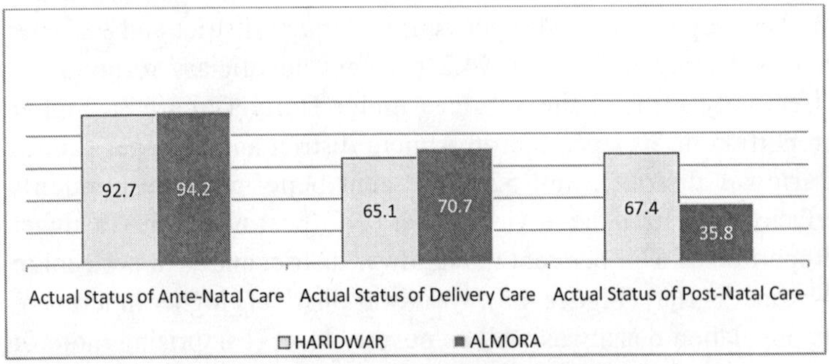

Figure 4.5: Actual Status of Maternal Health Care in Uttarakhand (Percentage Points) N= 173

With regard to ANC (Ante-natal care), the pattern of utilization showed a highest proportion with respect to undertaking the clinical examination (that is Haemoglobin test, Blood pressure test, Ultrasound, Weight, Urine test, Blood test, abdominal examination, and Breast examination) during their last pregnancy; followed by pregnancy registration and taking TT from JSY related centers; going for ANC check-ups under JSY; consuming IFA tablets during pregnancy;

counselling for institutional delivery by ASHA; and counselling for diet and rest during pregnancy. It was reported by 76.3 per cent beneficiary women that they received counselling for diet and rest during pregnancy and 79.2 per cent beneficiary women said that they had received counselling for institutional delivery by ASHA.

Out of a total 173 respondent beneficiary women 95.4 per cent (165) (88 in Haridwar and 77 in Almora) reported that they had registered their pregnancies under Janani Suraksha Yojna (JSY). Out of this, 63 per cent (72 in Haridwar and 37 in Almora) reported to have registered in the first Trimester of pregnancy, 32.9 per cent (16 in Haridwar and 41 in Almora) reported to have registered in the second Trimester of pregnancy, 1.7 per cent (1 in Haridwar and 2 in Almora) reported to have registered in the third Trimester of pregnancy; while 2.3 per cent did not respond on this matter.

Further, information on this issue revealed that 61.8 per cent (107) (80 in Haridwar, and 27 in Almora) had done their pregnancy registration with ASHA, 24.9 per cent women (43) (6 in Haridwar, and 37 in Almora) had done their pregnancy registration with ANM, 1.7 per cent (3) (3in Almora) had done their pregnancy registration directly in the PHC (Primary health Centre), 0.6 per cent (1) (1 in Haridwar) woman had done their pregnancy registration directly in the CHC (Community Health Centre), and 8.1 per cent women (14) (1 in Haridwar and 13 in Almora) had done their pregnancy registration directly in the DH (district hospital),while 2.9 per cent women (5) did not respond on this matter.

With regard to DC (Delivery care) the pattern of utilization showed a highest proportion with respect to undergoing institutional delivery; followed by receiving cash incentive for institutional delivery; benefitted by ASHA on escorting to health institution for delivery; incurring the emergency expenses. It was reported by 75 per cent beneficiary women that they were escorted by ASHA to the institution for delivery.

With regard to PNC (Post-natal care), the pattern of utilization showed a highest proportion with respect to staying in the health institution for more than 48 hours after delivery; followed by receiving counselling by ASHA /ANM for health and child care; and going for

PNC check-ups to the institution within 42 days after delivery. It was reported by 60.7 per cent beneficiary women that they were counselled by ASHA for mother and child health care after delivery.

Analysis of the above on the basis of geographical location revealed that a lower percentage of 67.1 per cent (55) in Almora district received counselling for diet and rest during pregnancy; in terms of social groups, it is SC-ST group that had a lowest percentage among the social groups.

In terms of geographical location 95.6 per cent (87) women in Haridwar district and all 82 in Almora district went for institutional delivery.

It was striking to observe that 76.9 per cent (70) respondents in Haridwar district and 43.9 per cent (36) in Almora district stayed in institution for more than 48 hours after their delivery. Social group wise 63.9 per cent (69) women from SC-ST group and 74.2 per cent (23) from OBC group stayed in institution for more than 48 hours after delivery.

4.4.1 Ante-Natal Care

Ante-natal care (ANC) on the first basis involves early registration of pregnancy for the purpose of preparing a woman for pregnancy and delivery. It comprises of examination, past delivery record, initial blood tests and immunisation. Antenatal care serves as an indicator of access as well as use of maternal health care during pregnancy. It involves at least three antenatal visits during a pregnancy period. This should begin as early in pregnancy as possible. IFA consumption by pregnant women is an indicator of quality of ANC, besides TT vaccination or Booster coverage. All pregnant women registered under JSY are recommended 100 IFA tablets, two TT immunizations in their first pregnancy and on subsequent pregnancies only a booster dose is sufficient. The respondent women beneficiaries were asked about the antenatal services utilized by them under Janani Suraksha Yojana and problems encountered.

4.4.1 a Facility of Early Registration

Task of registration under Janani Suraksha Yojana is vital in order to avail the benefits under this scheme, and more so for follow-up and monitoring of the activities. With regard to ANC (Ante-natal care), an analysis was done to understand the difficulties faced in availing the facility of Early Registration by the 173 selected beneficiary respondent women.

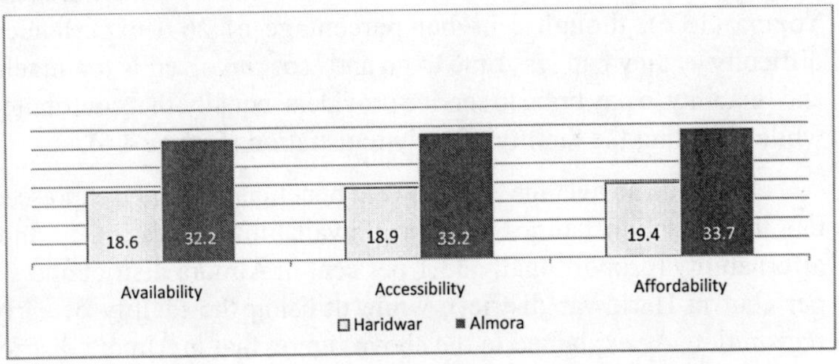

Figure 4.6: Problems Faced in Availing Facility of Early Registration (Percentage Points)

It was observed that on an average 25.1 per cent beneficiary women (a higher proportion of 32.4 per cent in Almora district than 18.6 per cent in Haridwar district) faced difficulty in terms of availability of early registration as maternal health service under JSY, overall a higher 26 per cent beneficiary women equally reported that lack of privacy in government health institution, non-availability of service providers on timely basis, and lack of experienced medical staff were the difficulties encountered while registering their pregnancy; while other difficulties included 'no posting of service providers', 'lack of hygiene in the health institution', 'medical instruments are old and do not function properly', 'service providers are not trustworthy' and distant health institutions - that contributed while availing the facility of early registration in both districts, but proportionally more in Almora district. On an average 25.7 per cent beneficiary women (proportionally 33.2 per cent in Almora district and 19 per cent in Haridwar district), faced difficulties in terms of accessibility of early registration as maternal health services under JSY, a highest percentage of 26.4 beneficiary women among other accessibility issues stated that government hospital care is time consuming while accessing the early registration facility, and other difficulties included 'service providers in the health institution use offensive language', 'service providers deny the health services', and 'inconvenient transportation'-that contributed while accessing the facility of early registration. On an average 26.2 per cent beneficiary women (proportionally 33.7 per cent in Almora district and 19.4 per cent in Haridwar district) faced difficulties in terms of affordability of early registration as maternal health services under Janani Suraksha Yojana (JSY), though a higher percentage of 26.6 experienced difficulty as they had less time to go and 'cost involved is too much' and 'inability to pay bribe to service providers' equally-that contributed while affording the facility of early registration **(Figure 4.6).**

Overall on an average 25.7 per cent beneficiary women expressed that they faced difficulties in terms of availability, accessibility, and, affordability (proportionally 33.1 per cent in Almora district and 19 per cent in Haridwar district), while utilising the facility of early registration. As explained in the above figure, that in Almora district the beneficiary women have more dependence on JSY services and therefore they access more as compared to Haridwar district. As a result they encounter much and feel the difficulties. On the contrary, since respondent women of Haridwar district do not access much so they do not experience difficulties.

4.4.1 b Availing IFA Tablets/TT Vaccination

With regard to ANC (Ante-natal care) an analysis was done to understand the difficulties faced in availing IFA tablets/TT vaccination by the 173 selected beneficiary women.

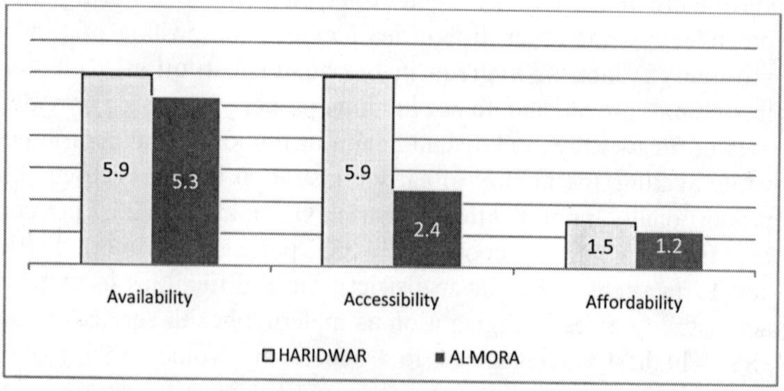

Figure 4.7: Problems Faced in Availing IFA Tablets/TT Vaccination (Percentage Points)

It was observed that on an average 4.6 per cent beneficiary women faced difficulty in terms of availability of IFA tablets/ TT vaccination under Janani Suraksha Yojna (JSY), wherein a higher 8.7 per cent beneficiary women reported that the 'institution was far away' and 'IFA tablets/TT vaccination was not available in the institution' equally and this was a difficulty while availing this facility, while other difficulties included 'service providers not coming on time', 'service providers are not posted' and 'staff are in-experienced'. On an average 3.1 per cent beneficiary women faced difficulty in terms of accessibility towards IFA tablets/ TT vaccination as maternal health services under JSY, wherein, a higher of 6.4 per cent beneficiary women reported that 'government hospital care is time consuming' while accessing this facility while other difficulties included 'denial of services', 'service providers are not trustworthy', and service providers use offensive language' experienced while accessing the facility of IFA tablets/TT vaccination. On an average 1.4 per cent beneficiary women faced difficulties in terms of affordability of IFA tablets/ TT vaccination as maternal health services under JSY, wherein, a higher percentage of 1.7 per cent beneficiary women reported that 'they did not have time to go' while others reported 'cost involved is too much' and 'they cannot pay service changes (that is bribe) to the service providers' experienced while affording the facility of IFA tablets/TT vaccination (**Figure 4.7**).

Overall, on an average only 3 per cent beneficiary women experienced difficulties in terms of availability, accessibility and affordability while availing the facility of IFA tablets/TT vaccination.

4.4.1. c ANC Checkups

With regard to ANC (Ante-natal care) an analysis was done to understand the difficulties faced while availing the facility of ANC check-ups by the 173 selected beneficiary women.

It was observed that on an average 3.5 per cent beneficiary women faced difficulties in terms of availability of ANC check-up service under Janani Suraksha Yojana, (JSY) a higher percentage of 10.4 per cent beneficiary women reported that the health institution being far away was a difficulty while availing ANC check-ups; whereas other difficulties included 'no privacy in institution', and 'instruments are old and are not functioning properly' equally; 'instruments are unhygienic', 'service provider are not posted', 'staff are in-experienced', and institutions are unhygienic'. On an average,2.4 per cent beneficiary women experienced difficulties in terms of accessibility of ANC check-ups as maternal health services under JSY, a higher percentage of 4.6 per cent revealed that as they had no problems during pregnancy, so they did not feel any need to go for routine check-ups; while other difficulties included 'offensive language used by service providers', 'government hospital care is time consuming', and 'they were denied check-ups and diagnosis by the service providers' also inconvenience in transportation' as well as 'service providers being non-trustworthy' equally. On an average just 0.6 per cent beneficiary women faced difficulties in terms of affordability of ANC check-ups as maternal health services under Janani Suraksha Yojana (JSY),with regard to high cost involvement', 'lack of time to go', 'inability to pay service charges (bribe) to service providers' in equal proportions (**Figure 4.8**). Overall, on an average only 2.2 per cent beneficiary women experienced difficulties in terms of availability, accessibility and affordability, while availing the facility of ANC –check-ups.

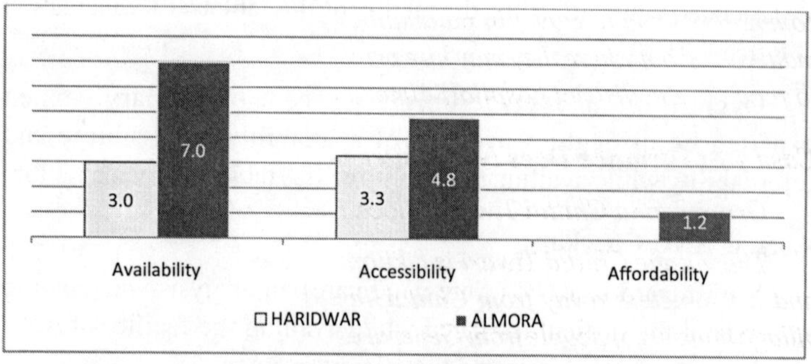

Figure 4.8: Problems Faced in Availing Facility of ANC Checkups (Percentage Points)

Case 4.7: Distance is a Struggle in Hill District

Village Balta; Block Hawal Bagh; District Almora

The village Papparshaili is around 5 kilometers away from Almora city. There is a small market in Papparshaili. Balta is 5 kilometers away from Papparshaili; yet, people from the village Balta often go to Papparshaili to get their ration. The road connecting the village to the market is in bad condition. It further deteriorated during disaster that took place in September 2010. There used to be a yard in the Balta village which was destroyed in the disaster that took place in September 2010. Around 20 out of the 30 men and women residing in this yard lost their lives during the calamity. The ANM Centre catering to this village is located in the district hospital, Almora. For vaccination and immunization the people from this village travel to Government School Balta, which is around 2 kilometers away from this village. Mostly scheduled caste people working as craftsmen are the major inhabitants of this village. The local people of Balta village grow vegetables and sell it in the Almora market. The residents of the village stated that the ASHA worker residing in Papparshaili never visits their village. They were of the belief that the ASHA worker should be selected from the residents of Balta village rather than from those in Papparshaili. Women in this village have to travel ten kilometers to Almora district hospital for child delivery and maternity services. Moreover, the pregnant women from general as well as schedule caste community have to travel in palanquin for 6 kilometers to reach the main road from where they may hire private vehicles or local carriages to reach to the district hospital, Almora for deliveries.

Case 4.8: Distance Does Not Matter to Some

Gram Sabha Chittai Tiwari; Block Hawalbagh, District Almora

The village Chittai Tiwari is 8 kilometers away from Almora city and 2 kilometers away from Chittai Temple. The population of this village consists of people from General as well as from Schedule Caste category. The main occupation of latter is craftsmanship. Because of its proximity to the city, the educational level of the village is comparatively better than other villages in vicinity. In terms of economic indicators, 75 per cent of the families are doing well while the rest 25 per cent are not so well off. The ANM Centre for the village is located 2 kilometers away while a subcenter exists within the village locality. The pharmacist is not there in the subcenter, while the ANM and the fourth class employees are available in this Sub-Centre. The women from the village use this facility for vaccination. JSY cards are also issued in this subcenter. However, a few people from the village go to District hospital for getting their JSY card made. Furthermore for child delivery and to avail maternity services people from the village go to the district hospital. The ASHA worker caters to the people in village, while her husband works with the local government office. The district hospital that caters to Chittai village is located 8 kilometers away and the locals therefore need to walk down for one and a half kilometer to reach the main road from where they need to take a private vehicle to reach to the district hospital. For a pregnant woman this is troublesome as during emergency or for access to immediate care and facilities, she is required to travel to reach the district hospital for delivery. Because of better educational and economic status, people in this village are well aware about the existence and benefits of JSY.

4.4.2 Delivery Care

Institutional delivery being the main approach for promoting safe motherhood, it is essential that all women should be encouraged to receive benefits of institutional care. With a view to support women from poor families to make way in public health institution for delivery, in low performing state like Uttarakhand, the remuneration of JSY should be made available to all women availing institutional delivery care in public health institutions like sub-centres, primary health centres, community health centres, and district hospitals.

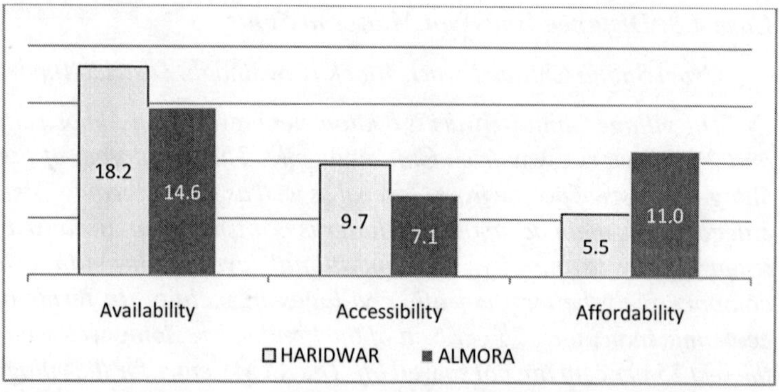

Figure 4.9: Problems Faced in Availing Facility of Institutional Delivery (Percentage Points)

The most immediate output expected from the JSY is an increase in institutional delivery. This has clearly happened as per available data sources like Health Management Information Systems (HMIS, 2009) and District Level Household and Facility Survey (DLHS-II, 2003; DLHS-III, 2008), showing a positive trend. With regard to institutional delivery, an analysis was done among the women for sample study to understand the difficulties faced in availing the facility of institutional delivery by the 173 selected beneficiary women. It was observed that on an average 16.5 per cent beneficiary women faced difficulties in terms of availability of institutional delivery as maternal health services under Janani Suraksha Yojna, (JSY), a higher 48.5 per cent beneficiary women (a higher proportion of 58.5 per cent in Almora district and 39.6 per cent in Haridwar district) reported that the health institution being far away and this is a difficulty while availing institutional delivery, while other difficulties included 'institutions are unhygienic' (a higher proportion of 26.4 per cent in Haridwar district and 6.1 per cent in Almora district), 'service providers do not come on time and are not posted'adequate in numbers, and 'instruments are old and not functioning properly', ' no privacy in the institutions', and 'staff are in-experienced'. On an average,7.9 per cent beneficiary women had faced difficulties in terms of accessing institutional delivery as maternal health care system under JSY, a higher of 19.7 per cent beneficiary women (a highest proportion of 27.5 per cent in Haridwar district and 11 per cent in Almora district) stated to have faced difficulty because care in hospital is time consuming, while other difficulties included, 'inconvenient transportation' (a higher proportion of 13.2 per cent in Haridwar district and 11 per cent in Almora district), 'offensive language used by service providers', 'service providers being non-trustworthy', 'service providers denied the delivery service and care', and 'inability to pay service charges or bribe' - that contributed while accessing institutional delivery care. On an average 6.3 per cent beneficiary women faced difficulties in terms of affording towards delivery care as maternal health services under Janani Suraksha Yojana (JSY), a higher of 10.4 per cent beneficiary women stated that problems such as 'inability to pay service charges to service providers', 'high cost involvement', (there was a higher proportion of 22 per cent in Almora district than 12.1 per cent in Haridwar district) alongwith, payment of bribe to the service providers, while other difficulties included, 'lack of time to go the institution for delivery'-that contributed while affording to the institutional delivery (**Figure 4.9**). During the field-visits it was noted that very few number of sub-centres had provided facilities for institutional deliveries and so it may not have been taken up in the sample area by the respondent women. On the other hand the common impression of sub-centres not being a favoured place of institutional delivery is confirmed here. Additionally, not all sub-centres are designated as place of institutional delivery.

Overall, on an average 10.2 per cent beneficiary women expressed difficulties in terms of availability (a higher proportion of 18.2 per cent in Haridwar district and 14.6 per cent in Almora district), accessibility (a higher proportion of 9.7 per cent in Haridwar district and 7.1 per cent in Almora district), and affordability (a lower proportion of 5.5 per cent in Haridwar district and 11 per cent in Almora district), while utilising the facility of institutional delivery. The cash benefit should be disbursed to the beneficiary women preferably at the institution. If ASHA is unable to arrange transport, disbursement of transport assistance should be done in the health centre as soon pregnant women get there and register for delivery. It should be the responsibility of ANM, MO, PHC/ASHA to take all proactive actions to ensure timely disbursement. So, it is required that the cash benefit be made available under this scheme and is used by the beneficiary for pregnancy related care especially at delivery time, and also for post natal care. According to the guidelines, payment to JSY beneficiary women delivering in a government facility should be paid at the institution itself through cheque. However, out of 173 beneficiary women 85.5 per cent reported that they received monetary incentive for their delivery in the government health institution as per the norms, thus pointing to a reasonably well-functioning scheme in this regard.

Case 4.9: Home Deliveries Due to Ill-Equipped Distant Sub-Centres; Still No Reported Case of Rs.500 Cash Incentive for Home Delivery

Tulsi Devi, wife of Ganga Ram; Village Taya; ASHA Worker; Block Sult; District Almora

JSY Survey was conducted in two Blocks of Almora Village. One is Hawalbagh which is next to Almora, second is Block Sult which is far away from Almora. The survey was conducted in 8 villages of Sult Block. However, out of these 8 villages, the situation of Taya village is different. This village is situated 10 kilometers far from Bhikyasen and to reach this village one has to climb 176 stairs. Once we reached this village after walking down one and a half kilometer we tried to contact ASHA Worker in the village. She informed that the government is running JSY and NRHM Scheme in the village but none of them is effective. Most of the deliveries in this village are done at home because the ANM Centre for this village is situated 25 kilometers away and is not adequately equipped for the purpose of child birth. The immunization of the pregnant women is done at the school 3 kilometers away and by the time the doctors reach the delivery is done at home itself. For the past one year, all the ten deliveries were conducted at home only in this village and none of the families have received financial aid of ₹ 500. The work area of the ASHA worker is also spread and she has to travel 3 kilometers through forest area to reach another village. For delivery the women from this village go to Matrojkhan or Ranikhet.

Case 4.10: Better Medical Services at Low Cost - Government Health Institutions are Better Compared to Private Health Institutions

Brajesh Devi, 26 Years, SC, wife of Shri Vikas; Village Panjanheri; Post Bhahdarabad; District Haridwar

While conducting the survey under the JSY study team reached the village Panjanheri where they met Smt Brajesh Devi, who stated that for her delivery when she visited the private hospital she could not get any proper treatment. Also the expenses related to delivery were too much and out of reach for a person like her. She informed that the third time she was pregnant, she got herself registered with the local ASHA worker. The ASHA worker provided her with iron tablets and help in getting immunized for tetanus. The ASHA worker also accompanied her to the government hospital, Haridwar thrice where she got her routine examination done including blood test, urine test, HIV test and all other diagnostic procedures. At the time of delivery too, the ASHA worker called the ambulance. Brajesh Devi stayed for three days in the hospital where she said that she never had any problems. She was dropped at her home by "Khushi Ki Sawari" provided under the scheme. When after a week she went to the hospital again for regular checkups she received the amount of Rs 1400/- incentive under the scheme. She feels that the JSY is a good initiative being taken by the government which is beneficial for poor people. She has been referring others too in the neighborhood to go the government hospital and avail all the benefits under the Scheme. Brajesh Devi was of the view that one can get better medical services at low cost in the government hospital therefore there is no need to refer to expensive private hospitals.

4.4.3 Post-Natal Care

Postnatal care is a necessary part of maternal care, to identify complications so that they can be treated early. PNC coverage is a pointer of access and use of health care after delivery. As a part of this, women should receive at least two postnatal care check-ups, to avoid and treat any complication. Postnatal care also involves counselling for diet for the mother and initiation of breastfeeding to the newborn within one-hour of delivery and its continuance for upto six months. Affordability is a major concern for the respondent women of Almora district both in terms of delivery care and postnatal care services mainly due to its difficult hilly terrain and transportation costs.

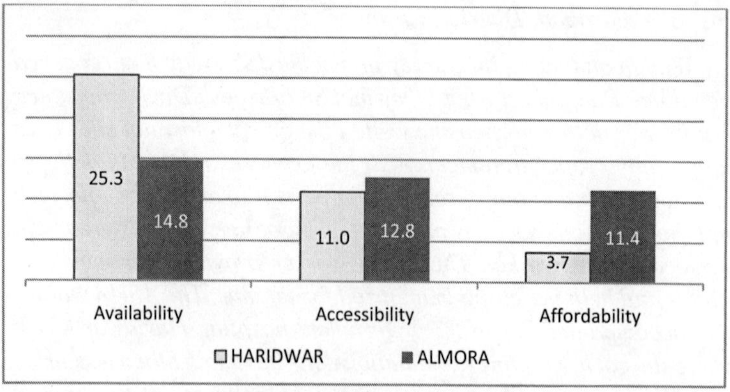

Figure 4.10: Problems Faced in Availing PNC Facility (Percentage Points)

With regard to PNC (Post-natal care) an analysis was done to understand the difficulties faced while availing the facility of Post-Natal Care by the 173 selected beneficiary respondent women. It was observed that on an average 20.3 per cent beneficiary women reported to face difficulties in terms of availability of Post-natal care as maternal health care service under Janani Suraksha Yojna, (JSY) a higher percentage of 52 per cent beneficiary women (54.9 per cent from Almora district and 49.5 per cent from Haridwar district) stated that the health institution was far away and this was a difficulty while availing PNC care, while other difficulties included 'institutions are unhygienic', 'service providers not coming on time', 'no privacy in the institution', 'service providers are not posted', 'instruments are old and not functioning properly', and 'staff are in-experienced'- that contributed to problems faced while availing PNC facilities. On an average 11.9 per cent beneficiary women faced difficulties in terms of accessibility of post-natal-care as an important part of maternal health care services under JSY, a higher percentage of 19.7 per cent beneficiary women (26.4 per cent in Haridwar district and 12.2 per cent in Almora district) stated to have faced difficulty because the care provided in government hospital is time consuming, while other difficulties included, 'inconvenience in transportation' (17.1 per cent in Almora district and 12.1 per cent in Haridwar district), and 'some felt that that they had no problem after pregnancy so there was no need to go for check-ups' (26.8 per cent in Almora district and just 3.3 per cent in Haridwar district), ' service providers used offensive language', 'service providers are not trustworthy', and they stated that they went to health institution for check-ups but were denied the service by the service providers-that contributed to problems while accessing PNC maternal health service. On an average 7.3 per cent beneficiary women faced difficulties in terms of affordability of post-natal-care as maternal health care services under JSY, a higher percentage of 8.6 per cent stated that they could not pay service charges to service providers, while other difficulties included, 'didn't have time to go', 'cost involvement is too much'—that contributed to difficulties while affording the maternal health care services.

Overall, on an average 13.2 per cent beneficiary women expressed difficulties faced in terms of availability (a higher proportion of

25.3 per cent in Haridwar district and 14.8 per cent in Almora district), accessibility (a higher proportion of 12.8 per cent in Almora district than 11 per cent in Haridwar district), and affordability (a higher proportion of 11.4 per cent in Almora district and just 3.7 per cent in Haridwar district), while utilising the facility of PNC (post–natal-care) (**Figure 4.10**).

4.5 Pregnancy Related Beliefs and Practices

From the above analysis , overall on an average basis, it can be noted that in terms of the three level of maternal health care services (Ante-natal-care, Delivery care, Post-natal-care) 21.5 per cent beneficiary women respondents faced difficulties in terms of availability, 15.5 per cent beneficiary women faced difficulties in terms of accessing the services, and 13 per cent beneficiary women faced difficulties in terms of affordability of the JSY services by the health institutions.

With regard to Ante-natal care (ANC) provided by the maternal health care services under Janani Suraksha Yojna (JSY), an analysis was done in order to understand the pregnancy related beliefs and practices among the 173 selected beneficiary respondent women. It was revealed that on an average the highest percentage of 19.6 per cent beneficiary women stated that they felt hesitant to take pregnancy related care from male service providers in the hospitals, 16.8 per cent beneficiary women stated that they were hesitant to share their pregnancy related issues with others,13.3 per cent beneficiary women stated that according to their family tradition and practices delivery has to happen within their own home, 8.6 per cent beneficiary women stated that the institutional delivery and care do not follow many of their family customs and practices; while other beliefs and practices included-dais/TBAs are competent than doctors in handling pregnancy issues (5.8 per cent); sharing of pregnancy issues with strangers brings bad luck during delivery (5.2 per cent) expressed their their concern; their in-laws did not like them to go to government health care services (3.5 per cent); pregnancy is a natural phenomenon so it does not require any institution care (2.9 per cent) and pregnancy related check-ups in hospitals leads to birth of girl child (1.2 per cent).From the above information on an overall basis, it was observed that on an average

8.5 per cent beneficiary respondents women under Janani Suraksha Yojana (JSY) believed in their own pregnancy related customs and practices.

Case 4.11: Negligence of Family and their Mindset Leading to Still Birth

Shahzadi, 5th Pass, wife of Shri Waseem Rao; OBC Muslim; Village Ibrahimpur; Post Bhahdarabad; District Haridwar

Smt Shahazdi is a resident of Ibrahimpur village. She got married to Mr Rao one year ago. When the study team enquired about the JSY Scheme she initially claimed that she knew nothing about the Scheme. Later she shared about her pregnancy few months ago, and she informed us that she had got herself registered with the help of Aanganwadi worker. She received the iron tablets through the ASHA worker who also provided her with Tetanus vaccination and helped her in getting her routine examination done. During the time of her delivery the ASHA worker called for the ambulance and took her to the community health centre Baghdadabad. However, the staff of this centre were on strike that day. The doctor there therefore referred this case to district hospital, Haridwar. The doctor was rude to them. The ASHA worker took her to the district hospital in Haridwar. However, the staff there asked them to go for medical examination once again and send them back. The doctors there again were rude and therefore her husband too got irritated. They got her back to the community health centre, Bahdarabad. The strike was over by then. They met the doctor who told them that an operation is required to be done, however, for that there was no facility available at the centre and he refused to admit her there. An argument took place between the doctor and Shahzadi's husband.

The family then got her back saying that whatever may happen they will not go the hospital and the baby will be delivered at home. She was bleeding profusely for three days and was feeling weak and dizzy. Though at this last stage, her mother-in-law told her husband that Shahzadi should be taken to private hospital, however, the husband got a midwife (Dai) at home. The dai conducted the home delivery and Shahzadi gave birth to a still baby. Her parents had also advised her to go for operation during her second trimester and that she should have been precautious. She herself had requested her husband to take her to private hospital but he didn't pay heed to her requests. Now she believes that it was not only the negligence on the part of the government but it was also the fault of her husband's too. If she would have received timely and proper care, her child would have been alive. According to her, the ASHA worker has fully cooperated with her and she availed her of the facilities under the JSY Scheme. However, it is because of negligence by her family and their conservative mindset which is responsible for this tragic incident, when JSY is a scheme for saving the lives of mothers and new-born from the causes related to delivery.

4.6 General Awareness and Perception about JSY

Singh et al. (2006) carried out a study in the tribal belt of Mizoram and Tripura, to assess the awareness and utilization of reproductive and child health services among women. Study reported on the demographic objectives, notably about the increasing contraceptive prevalence rates and reducing fertility of Indian family welfare programme as policy drawback in catering to the health needs of women. Apart from policy structure the study also found variety of socio-cultural and biological factors responsible for poor reproductive health in India. Study further revealed about inadequate delivery system to cater to the needs of secluded, shy and devalued women. With regard to the present study, evidence remains inadequate as to the degree to which women are correctly informed about the eligibility

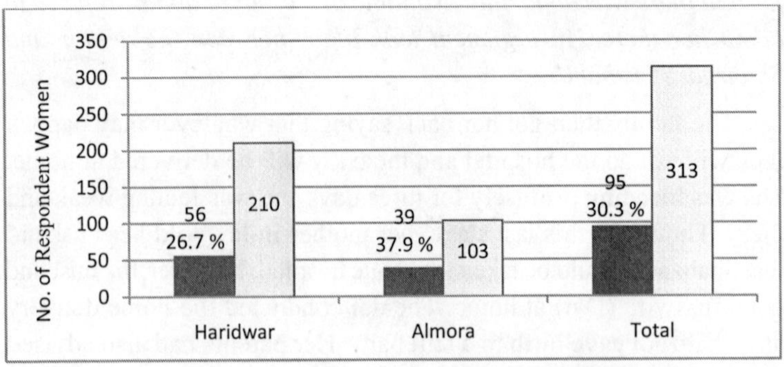

Figure 4.11: General Awareness About JSY.

criteria for gaining from the scheme and the monetary and non-monetary entitlements under it. However, this concern to some extent also suggest that awareness may not have been comprehensive.

Findings indicate that regardless of the place of residence, on an overall basis out of 313 study respondents, nearly 30 per cent (95) respondents (72 from rural settings and 23 from urban settings) (56 from Haridwar and 39 from Almora) were found aware and informed about JSY and its benefits, and nearly 8 per cent were found not sure about JSY, while 62 per cent respondents had no acquaintance with JSY and its benefits (**Figure 4.11**). Moreover, more than half of the women who had heard about the scheme and generally aware of this were more rural than urban women from plain areas (Haridwar) than from the hills (Almora).The figure presents findings on women's awareness of the JSY in general. Although sixty-two per cent respondent women informed that they did not have proper information and awareness of the JSY, fewer (30 per cent) were correctly informed about the criteria for benefiting from the scheme, as evident from above figure.

The perception of respondent women on various dimensions and of the type of facilities where they could deliver in order to receive JSY benefits, perception about the Janani Suraksha Yojna, among the 173 study respondents who utilized the maternal health services under JSY (Janani Suraksha Yojana) largely revealed among them 94.8 per cent believed that pregnancy registration in first trimester of pregnancy is important for safe pregnancy; 89.6 per cent believed that consumption of IFA tablets are helpful for pregnant women; 95.4 per cent believed that TT vaccination is helpful during pregnancy; 91.3 per cent beneficiaries believed that ANC check-ups in the institutions are helpful to pregnant mother for monitoring her pregnancy; 99.4 per cent beneficiaries believed that institutional delivery is safe for pregnant mothers; 87.8 per cent beneficiary women believed that staying for minimum 48 hours in hospital after delivery helps women to recover her health.

An analysis of awareness about ANC (Ante-natal care) was on an average 77.9 per cent; awareness about DC (Delivery care) was 68.8 per cent; awareness about PNC (Post-natal care) was

75.4 per cent. With regard to ANC (Ante-natal care) the highest awareness was found about TT vaccination that is provided for pregnant mother; and lowest awareness was found about the micro-plan that is developed by ASHA/ANM. Micro-birth plan is a means for efficient coordination of all the activities principally involves essential activities and would be performed by whom, within the desired time period. Micro-birth planning comprises of dialogue and deciding the date of next check-up, place of next check-up, place of delivery, expected date of delivery, and place of referral, in case of complications. Further, this micro-birth plan needs to be prepared by the ANM, or ASHA under its components like dates of 3 ANC and TT injection and after ensuring these are done, identifying health centre for all referral, identifying delivery place, inform expected delivery date, etc.

Observations on the attitudes and perception towards ANC (Ante Natal Care) among the total 173 sample beneficiary respondents in the state of Uttarakhand were found positive among 92.8 per cent beneficiary women on an average basis. Of this a maximum proportion of positive attitude and perception was that they believed that TT vaccination is helpful during pregnancy period (95.4 per cent); followed by 94.8 per cent (they believe that pregnancy registration in first trimester is important for pregnancy); 91.3 per cent (they believe that ANC check-ups in institutions are helpful to pregnant mother in order to keep a close watch and monitor her own pregnancy; and 89.6 per cent (they believe that IFA tablets are helpful for pregnant women).

Analysis of awareness about DC (Delivery care) revealed that the highest awareness among respondent beneficiaries was that the institutional delivery is safe for pregnant mothers; whereas the lowest awareness was found regarding untied fund which is available with ANM and that which can be advanced to ASHA to meet urgent expenses during delivery.

With regard to PNC (Post Natal Care) among the respondent beneficiaries the highest level of awareness was about staying minimum 2 days in hospital after delivery helps women to recover her health; whereas the lowest level of awareness was noted with regard to beneficiary women who are entitled for counselling from ASHA /ANM for their own health and also child care after delivery.

Therefore, on an overall basis, on an average 74.1 per cent respondent beneficiary women were found to be aware with regard to ANC (ante-natal care), DC (delivery care) and PNC (post-natal care). Thus, overall, the findings underline that quality of health services received by women during pregnancy, delivery and the postpartum period remains poor. For instance among JSY beneficiaries, few women had received, during antenatal services, complete information about complications that may occur during pregnancy as well as about birth preparedness. A comprehensive evaluation of Janani Suraksha Yojana is yet to come to know how far this programme has achieved its goal. However, studies conducted on this programme in different parts of India in different time period have two broad focuses, first, is its implementation process; and second is to measure the progress of maternal health goals of the mission such as increased institutional care and delivery as well as decreased maternal mortality. There is no study available to describe what and how different factors and variables have affected the progress of JSY. This chapter indicates that appropriate practices in labour and delivery were rarely followed in the study settings at the facility level. Limited access to transportation, medicines and other supplies as well as to a courteous and clean facility for delivery remain other major concerns.

Chapter - 5

Critique of Service Providers and Health Institutions in Uttarakhand

The first section of this chapter provides the findings about the role of service providers in the JSY scheme vis-à-vis support provided by them to the beneficiary mothers in their respective areas of operation; in the second part of the chapter, efforts have been made to look into the functioning and experiences of the health institutions and services at the levels of sub-centre, primary health centre, community health centre, and district hospitals.

Health service providers are the main actors under the National Rural Health Mission provided at the village level to the district and the state level. As such, they have a vital role to play in implementing the JSY scheme till the grassroots level. In order to implement the scheme, Janani Suraksha Yojana introduced the ASHA, a trained female community health activist, who is responsible to work as an interface between the community and the public health system. She is selected from the village itself and is accountable to perform a vital role in the milieu of maternal and child health. With regard to JSY she is responsible to facilitate delivery in a government medical facility. The assigned role of ASHA is to identify the pregnant woman within the village, and ensure that this woman receives prenatal care, spot the functioning government medical facility where this pregnant woman can deliver her baby, arrange for transport, accompany the woman till the medical institution and stay with her till the time of discharge after delivery. According to JSY guidelines, she is to be paid ₹ 600 per delivery only if she facilitates delivery in a government medical facility. Later she is also responsible for arranging immunisation for the new born as well as postnatal care for the mother.

5.1 Selected Service Providers

The sample covered in the state of Uttarakhand also includes several stakeholders associated with the scheme such as Auxiliary Nurse Midwife (ANMs), Accredited Social Health Activists (ASHA), Nurses, and Doctors, besides the beneficiary women of JSY (Janani Suraksha Yojana). On an overall basis 58 of these service providers were interviewed, out of which 25 (43 per cent) were from Hill (Almora) district (20 ASHAs and 5 ANMs) and 33 (57 per cent) service providers from Plains (Haridwar) district (24 ASHAs, 5 ANMs, 2 Nurses, and 2 Doctors) were selected for the study. With regards to the social group of these above mentioned service providers, out of 25 service providers from Hills (Almora) district a higher proportion of 15 belonged to General category, 5 belonged to SC (Scheduled castes) category, 2 belonged to OBC (Other Backward Caste) category while 3 of them did not reveal anything about their social group. On the other hand, in the Plains (Haridwar) district out of 33 selected service providers, a higher proportion of 13 were from SC (Scheduled Caste) group, 10 were from General category, 8 were from OBC (Other Backward Caste) group, and just one belonged to ST (scheduled Tribe) category.

An effort was made to enquire as to how far these service providers succeeded in motivating pregnant women for institutional delivery. In the Hill (Almora) district 20 (80 per cent) out of 25 service providers revealed that they could motivate nearly all the pregnant women in their area towards institutional delivery; while in the Plains (Haridwar) district out of 33 service providers 27 (82 per cent) revealed that they could motivate nearly all the pregnant women towards institutional delivery.

BPL pregnant women, 19 years and above, who desire to deliver at home is entitled to monetary assistance of ₹ 500/- per delivery; this cash assistance is obtainable only upto 2 live births and is paid at the time of delivery or within a week prior to delivery by ANM or ASHA. The underlying purpose is that beneficiary would be able to use this money for her care or any incidental expenses of delivery. It is crucial to have a BPL certificate to access JSY benefits. However, it is the responsibility of ANM, ASHA to counsel the pregnant woman to deliver in a health institution. With such perspective regarding home delivery, 3 out of 25 service providers in Hills (Almora) district and 20 out of 33 service providers in Plains (Haridwar) district stated that in their area women prefer for home delivery instead of delivery in government institutions. Exploring the reasons for preference for home delivery, one service provider from Almora district and 15 from Haridwar district stated that the in-laws of those pregnant women impose restrictions on them to go for institutional delivery. Twenty-four out of 25 service providers in Hills (Almora) district and 26 out of 33 in Plains (Haridwar district) claimed that they were adequately trained to carry out their job in general. However further it was reported that 24 out of 25 service providers in Hills (Almora district) and 23 out of 33 service providers in Plains (Haridwar) felt that they were trained to carry out ante-natal care (ANC) as well as post natal care (PNC) for the pregnant women before and after delivery, respectively. However, it was very critical to note that only 5 out of 25 (that is 20 per cent) selected service providers in Hills (Almora district) and 9 out of 33 (27 per cent) selected service providers in Plains (Haridwar district) reported that they were trained to carry out safe delivery.

In Hills (Almora district) a highest proportion of 21 service providers out of 25, provide each ante-natal care (ANC) services as well as post natal care (PNC) services to the JSY beneficiary women before and after delivery. Whereas in Plains (Haridwar district) a higher proportion of 18 service providers out of 33 selected service providers provide ante-natal care (ANC) services; and an equal proportion of 13 service providers out of 33 selected service providers normally provide post natal care (PNC) services each at the homes of the beneficiary women and at the Sub-Centre level.

In the Hills (Almora district) the highest proportion of 20 out of 25 selected service providers and in Plains (Haridwar district) a higher proportion of 27 out of 33 selected service providers reported that JSY beneficiary women belonging to Scheduled Caste (SC) social category, generally, approach their Sub-Centres irrespective of study sample respondents alone in order to avail ante-natal care (ANC) services as well as post natal care (PNC) services (**Figure 5.1**). Further, with regards to the religious category, a higher proportion of 22 out of

25 selected service providers in the Hills (Almora district) and 24 out of 33 selected services providers in the Plains (Haridwar district) reported that JSY beneficiary women belonging to Hindu religious category approach the service providers at the Sub-Centre level to avail the ante-natal care (ANC) services as well as post-natal care (PNC) services. The data quoted in this figure do not necessarily correspond to the social categories of selected sample respondents for the purpose of the present research study.

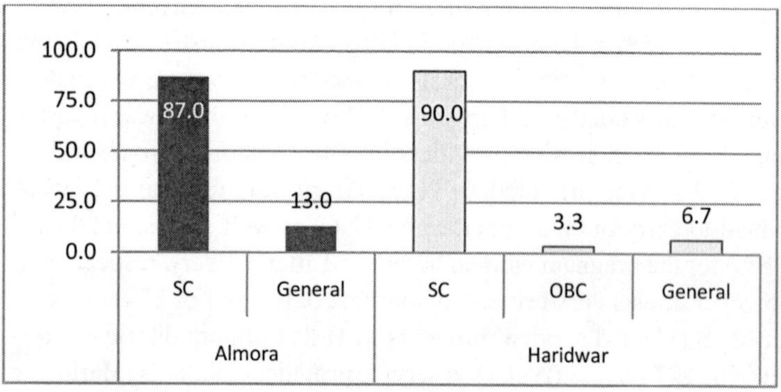

Figure 5.1: Social Category of Beneficiary (Sub Centre Level) (Valid Percentage)

In the Hills (Almora district) two ANMs out of selected 25 service providers and in the Plains (Haridwar district) one ANM out of selected 33 service providers reported that they do conduct delivery at their Sub-Centres. However, it was reported that 5 out of selected 25 service providers in the Hills (Almora district) and 10 out of 33 selected service providers in the Plains (Haridwar district) reported that by and large nearly the basic facilities and equipments required for normal delivery were available in their Sub-Centres.

In the Hills (Almora district) and in the Plains (Haridwar district) all the selected 5 ANMs from each of these two districts reported that they have used the untied fund during the last year. These ANMs reported that this untied fund was mainly utilized for the emergency expenses of the villagers in general in their respective areas.

These ANMs are provided with First Aid Kit, Delivery Kit, Sufficient medicines, Referral slips, sufficient space provided in their cabin to talk about private issues of patients, separate private space for pregnancy check-ups, literature for community meetings, untied-fund for emergency use, guidance and support from experts, training/exposure on any new subject, ASHAs for their use, stationary and diary for record keeping.

Assessment of the kind of activities conducted by Health Department during the last one year in order to generate awareness among the people about the JSY (Janani Suraksha Yojana) Scheme, out of the selected 25 service providers in Hills (Almora district) and 33 service providers in Plains (Haridwar district) – use of posters and pamphlets (one in Almora district, 16 in Haridwar district); use of street theatres (4 in Haridwar district); through advertisements by Televisions or Radio (2 in Almora district), through community level meetings (15 in Almora district and 20 in Haridwar district); Others (8 in Almora district, 2 in Haridwar district).

5.2 Perception of Health Service Providers on Utilization Level of Maternal Health Services

The perception of health service providers was recorded in order to understand the utilization level of maternal health services in their respective work areas included in this study. An assessment of the perception of these JSY related selected service providers (25 selected service providers in Hills (Almora district) and 33 selected service providers in Plains (Haridwar district) about the utilization level of the maternal health care services in their respective areas revealed that, overall, in terms of ante-natal care (ANC) utilisation level was 48.1 per cent which is very good and good (48.5 per cent in Almora and 47.7 per cent in Haridwar district) while it was 1.9 per cent average and low (1.5 per cent in Almora district and 2.3 per cent in Haridwar district). In terms of delivery care (DC) on an overall basis the maternal health care service utilization level was very good and good 47.4 per cent (48 per cent in Almora district and 46.9 per cent in Haridwar district), while it was 2.5 per cent of average and low level (2 per cent in Almora district and 3 per cent in Haridwar district). Lastly, in terms of post-natal care (PNC) the level of maternal health care service utilization was reflected as 44.7 per cent (41 per cent in Almora district and 48.4 per cent in Haridwar district), while it was 5.3 per cent of average and low level (9 per cent in Almora district and 1.5 per cent in Haridwar district.

Table 5.1: Main Reasons behind Low Utilisation of Janani Suraksha Services in Hills (Almora District) and Plains (Haridwar District) of Uttarakhand

Hills (Almora district)	*Plains (Haridwar district)*
ASHA (general category social group) said that they have not faced any difficulty till then in their pregnancy so they did not realise the importance of the routine checkups and other counselling related to maternal health care services and safe motherhood provided by JSY.	ASHA (OBC social group) at Sub-Centre Katarpur revealed that female doctor not available when they go to the hospital.
ASHA of Barkinda Salt also revealed that they do not face any difficulty that's why they do not often go to the maternal health institution for routine checkups.	One BAMS doctor in CHC Bahadarabad stated that if there is not much problem and only haemoglobin level is low, so they do not feel the need to utilise other services, they manage on their own.
ASHA at Sub-Centre level of maternal health institution revealed that the hospital is far-off and also doctors are not available.	ASHA (scheduled caste social category) of Sub-Centre Jagjeetpur told that IFA tablets consumption leads into vomiting, sleepiness, and dizziness. Also people don't pay serious attention on needed care after delivery.
ANM (general category social group) of Sub-Centre (Ramna) level of health institution revealed that there is a lack of awareness among women about safe motherhood and institutional delivery.	ASHA of Chanderpuri said it is the family members and relatives who discourage the women to go to hospital for checkups. Also due to distance factor they express their inability to reach the hospital.
ASHA (general category social group) said there are no sufficient facilities for institutional delivery.	ASHA (general category social group) at Panjanhedi revealed that government works carelessly and their works are not done on time, in terms of provision of medicines, diagnostic check-ups, provision of transporttation before and after delivery on timely basis.
ASHA (General category social group) of Sub-Centre said that when there are no problems in pregnancy or delivery and everything goes normal naturally.	ASHA (Scheduled Caste social category) Panjadhedi said it is due to non-availability of injections and medicines.

(Contd...)

ASHA (General category social group) of Dwarahat revealed that only when they face any difficulty after delivery they go to the institution otherwise not. Also no information is provided to ASHA after delivery or even after check-ups in the institution.	Two ASHAs (one General category and one OBC social group) of CHC Laksar revealed that the honorarium of ASHA should be increased. The government employees of JSY demand money for delivering their services. Also ASHAs are asked to pay for the medicines they are provided with.
ASHA (OBC social group) of Nakuta, Beskhet said that they do not have any awareness or any information about the check-up even after delivery as well as about post-natal care. They do not require this care because they have never experienced this post-natal care of maternal health service.	ANM (General category social group) of Sub-Centre Bahadurpur Jat revealed that the Sub-Centre should be built-up properly. Trained Dai (TBA) should be made available, and also their honorarium should be increased.
ASHA (General category social group) of Kwairala Salt also revealed that only when they face any difficulty after delivery they go to the institution not otherwise.	The staff Nurse (OBC social group) in CHC Laksar reported that there is a need for bed and beddings in their CHC. She also stated that the honorarium for ASHA must be increased. The medicines as well as injections must be made available from time to time.
ASHA (Scheduled Caste social group) of District Hospital, Almora said that the medical staff and people there do not give sufficient time and attention to pregnant women.	Two more ASHAs (both general category social group) of Laksar revealed that the honorarium of ASHA should be increased. ASHA who escorts the pregnant woman for institutional delivery should be provided with stay facility along with the pregnant woman.

An analysis of some of main reasons behind (low utilization of JSY services as reported by the selected 25 service providers in Hills (Almora district) and selected 33 service providers in Plains (Haridwar district) are mentioned in **Table 5.1** above:

Some of the commonly observed deficiencies and complications among pregnant women include: anaemia, swelling, weakness, problems of high blood pressure, blood discharge, vomiting, very less interval between delivery and the birth of previous baby, calcium deficiency, non-consumption of healthy and nutritious food, acidity and pain (as reported by the selected service providers in Almora district); and; anaemia, swelling in feet, problems of high blood pressure, weakness, calcium deficiency, low haemoglobin, jaundice, and headache (as reported by the selected service providers in Haridwar district).

5.3 Challenges of JSY Service Providers

An assessment was done to understand the different challenges and problems faced by the selected service providers in implementing ante-natal care (ANC), post-natal care (PNC) and delivery services in Uttarakhand **(Figure 5.2).** In this regards, they revealed some challenges faced by them in implementation of JSY services overall which was at a higher level of 67.4 per cent in the plains (Haridwar district) than 48.1 per cent in the hills (Almora district), these percentage points were disaggregated in terms of – both high work load among women (68.45); and less importance given towards women's health within their families (68.45); lack of awareness among people (68.05); women feeling shy to share their pregnancy related matters (65.95); inconvenient transportation system (64.1); distance of health institutions (63.45); insufficient cash incentive (61); women having strong faith in the traditional care (60); women's carelessness towards their own health (55.95); pregnant women believing more on traditional birth attendant (dais) (55.65); customary practices of their own community (49.2); high cost of accessing maternal health care (47.5); women following their religions practices (41.25) as well as communication problem between beneficiary and health provider (39.2).

In case of hills (Almora district) highest percentage points were accorded to the top four factors that included-insufficient cash incentive (68.4 per cent), followed by less importance to women's health in their own family and also high workload among women (65 per cent each), and women feeling shy to share their pregnancy related matters (60 per cent).

In case of plains (Haridwar district) the top four factors having highest percentage points were accorded to–women believing more on traditional birth attendant (Dais) (81.3 per cent), followed by inconvenient in transportation and lack of awareness among people (78.2 per cent each) and women having strong faith in traditional care (75 per cent).

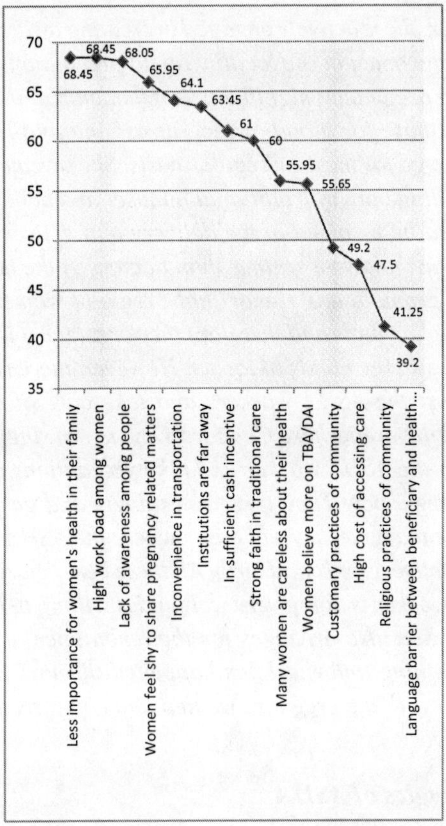

Figure 5.2: Challenges Faced by JSY Service Providers in Implementing ANC, DC, PNC Services (Percentage Points)

Case 5.1: Efforts of ASHA and Traditional Mindset of Communities

Chandra Devi, 8th Pass, wife of Shri Shyam Lal; ASHA Worker; Saini Caste; Village Ibrahimpur; Post Chandarpuri Bangar; Block Khanpur; District Haridwar

Chandra Devi is a resident of Village Chandarpuri Bangar and is the ASHA worker for the village who is doing her work with sincerity and integrity in spite of all ups and downs in life. Her husband too helps her in serving the community. He is educated till tenth class.

According to her, she is actively engaged in creating awareness among all the pregnant women in the locality about precautions and diet to be taken during pregnancy, significance of immunization and routine tests including those for blood, urine, ultrasound and HIV test and motivate them to go for these on regular basis. She revealed that many people in the village are of traditional mindset and believe that only midwives should be involved in the delivery and delivery practices. These people trust midwives rather than doctors in the hospital. The midwives also promote this rumor that pregnant women never get good care in the hospitals and therefore they create suspicion against medical services in the minds of locals. However, there is a group of people who trust the ASHA workers and take care of their family accordingly. In the area where Chandra Devi is working, most of the people listen to the ASHA worker and take precautions accordingly during their pregnancy. They take iron tablets and get themselves immunized. The team met several cases where the ASHA worker has helped during delivery and child birth. All these beneficiaries informed that the ASHA worker is doing very well and is willing to help women day and night. She also arranges for the ambulance at the time of delivery and nothing untoward has happened till now. She stays in the hospital too with the pregnant women and comforts them during the time of delivery.

Case 5.2: Struggles of ASHA

Mumtaz Jahan, 10th Pass; ASHA Worker; Muslim Community; District Almora

Mumtaz Jahan is a resident of Almora. She is a mother of two kids. According to her she is employed as an ASHA worker in a city where most of the people are educated and medical facilities are available for women easily. This is the major reason for which people do not call the ASHA worker even though she maintains regular contact with pregnant women for 9 months. During the time of delivery these women call up and go for child birth on their own. The ASHA worker is later informed about the child birth. Therefore, the ASHA worker's role is not recognised and the doctors claim the case as their own. And the cases which ASHA worker refers to the hospital for delivery end up in vain, as the hospital staff including the doctors and nurses ask for bribes after the delivery. The people from well to do family pay some amount, however, people who are not economically sound cannot do so. The hospital staffs therefore do not take care of these people properly. Once the women received the entitlement under JSY, they end up paying this money to the hospital staff. The situation is aggravated when the poor people are asked to pay. Mumtaz Jahan goes on to state that the district hospital lacks the arrangement for ASHA workers to stay at night. Now they are planning to convert the morgue to the rooms for the ASHA workers for this purpose.

Thus, some of the most important problems and delays in accessing health services during delivery were associated with the time taken in identifying and understanding the problem, arranging for the transport, travelling time involved, and delay in receiving medical attention and services even after reaching the place of delivery.

By and large it was reported by all the selected service providers (25 in Almora district and 33 in Haridwar district) that included ASHA, ANM, Nurses as well as Doctors that there has been an increase in utilization of different maternal health care services under JSY by the women of belonging to different communities both in Almora district ('yes' by 92 per cent and 'to some extent' by 8 per cent of the health service providers) in Almora district) as well as Haridwar district ('yes' by 78.8 per cent and 'to some extent' by 21.2 per cent of the health service providers).

5.4 Response of Health Service Providers on Institutional Deliveries

One of the imperative components of the Janani Suraksha Yojana is to provide monetary incentive to those mothers who deliver in an accredited institution. The guidelines of this scheme make provisions for such payment to all women beneficiaries delivering in a government health institution or even in those private institutions or facilities that are accredited under this scheme. Overall perception of the sample respondents revealed that on an overall basis 75.8 per cent of respondents stated that the cash incentive under Janani Suraksha Yojana plays a major role towards institutional delivery (96 per cent in Almora district and 85.9 per cent in Haridwar district).

The extent of success of the JSY programme can be evaluated by the proportion of all the deliveries conducted in the government health facility accredited under the scheme or even in the private health institutions. A probe whether Janani Suraksha Yojana has substantially increased institutional delivery in the selected two districts of Uttarakhand revealed that on an overall basis 96.35 per cent respondents reported that institutional delivery has substantially increased in Uttarakhand (95.8 per cent in Almora district and 96.9 per cent in Haridwar district) due to implementation of this scheme in general.

Analysis of the reasons that contributed as to know why Janani Suraksha Yojana did not succeed towards increased institutional delivery; out of 58 service providers a highest of 34 respondents stated that it was due to low awareness; followed by shortage of health institutions (11); shortage of health professionals (7); low level of quality care (5); health system is not woman friendly (3); and high cost of services (2). These reported grounds of mothers in Uttarakhand indicate that importance on proper planning for institutional delivery is given in the programme.

Therefore, complete awareness of the role of ASHA is limited; among those who reported awareness, the most generally known responsibilities of the ASHA comprised of facilitating three antenatal check-ups, giving advice about institutional delivery and escorting women to a health facility for delivery. Although those women in rural as well as in urban areas who had heard about the ASHA, it was observed that they were less likely to have awareness about the crucial role and responsibility of ASHAs as arranging transport facility to reach a health facility for institutional delivery and also her post-natal visits within one week of delivery. Therefore, it can be stated that proper awareness of Janani Suraksha Yojana aiming to promote safe motherhood through institutional delivery which is the need of the hour and its provisions like 108 ambulance service, besides this particular nutritional supplementation is limited; all women were found not aware of the ambulance service.

Attitude of service providers towards vulnerable group is an important aspect in order to motivate them for institutional care. Women especially from weaker sections of society face ill-treatment and were un-welcomed in health institutions. According to a study conducted by Yusuf et al. (2009) in two Muslim concentrated communities of Delhi to investigate effects of privatization of reproductive and child health services on Muslim women, the study revealed that there is strong intent to seek care, women often reach public health care facilities but are unable to utilize the services due to the dismal state of functioning such as - lack of privacy, lack of personnel, shortage of equipment or drugs, and overcrowding. In case of the urban poor slum dwelling women, the inability to access and utilize health services arise variously out of ignorance, cost of travelling to these institutions, negative attitude of health workers to urban slum clientele and inefficient functioning.

5.5 Selected Health Institutions

National Rural Health Mission looks for providing effective health services to the populace in rural sector having pathetic public health indicators and/or dismal infrastructures. With regard to such a situation, the Indian Public Health Standards (IPHS) were published and were made available in 2007 for Sub-Centres, Primary Health Centres (PHCs), Community Health Centres (CHCs), Sub-District and District Hospitals, which were used as the reference point for public health care infrastructure planning and upgradation for quality improvement of health care delivery in India. The following Table 5.2 provides data on main health infrastructures in position and what is required in Uttarakhand and demographic indicators are as follows comparative to the country:

Table 5.2: Health Infrastructure of Uttarakhand

Particulars	*Required*	*In position*	*Shortfall*
Sub-Centre	2341	1848	493
Primary Health Centre	351	257	94
Community Health Centre	87	59	28

(*Source*: RHS Bulletin, March 2012, M/O Health & F.W., GOI)

- Sub-Centre (SC)

The Sub-Centres are vital peripheral institutions for providing primary health care to the people and play a significant role in the implementation of Janani Suraksha Yojana at the grass-root level aiming to provide best level of quality services that meets the requirements of its beneficiaries. The present level of performance of the Sub-Centres is much below the expectations, as per RHS data (2012) of MoHFW states that the number of Sub-Centres fall short by 493 in Uttarakhand.

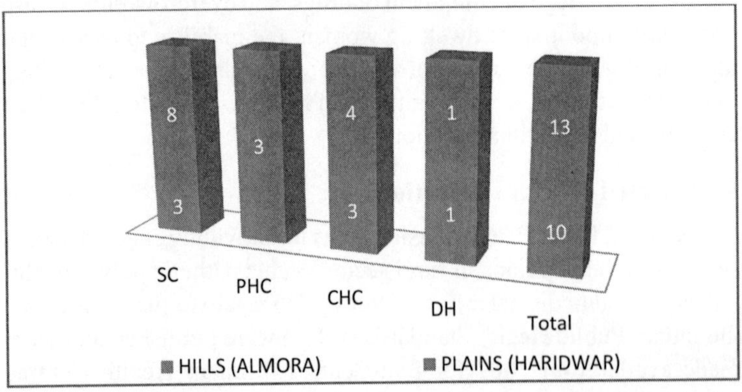

Figure 5.3: Numbers of Sample Health Institutions in Uttarakhand

At the Sub-Centre (SC) level, overall a sample of eleven maternal health institutions (3 in Almora and 8 in Haridwar) were surveyed in Uttarakhand. The three Sub-Centres in Hill district (Almora) included SC Daulaghat, SC Kwairala Salt and SC Ramna; and the eight selected Sub-Centre in Plain district (Haridwar) included SC Bahadurpur Jat, SC Govardhanpur, SC Jagjeetpur, SC Karanpur, SC Katarpur, SC Khanpur, SC Shahpur, Sheetla Kheda and SC Sikandarpur Laksar **(Figure 5.3).**

With regard to availability of human resources at the Sub-Centre level, it was reported that all the Sub-Centres had ANMs; none of the Sub-Centres in Almora district or in Haridwar district was having male health worker; 9 Sub-Centres reported to have (Dais) trained birth attendants; all Sub-Centres reported to have ASHAs.

With regard to availability of infrastructures at the Sub-Centre level, it was reported that 5 Sub-Centres had waiting room area; 5 Sub-Centres had labour room; 9 Sub-Centres had clinic room; 8 Sub-Centres had examination room; 3 Sub-Centres had IPD ward; 4 Sub-Centres had residence for ANMs; 9 Sub-Centres had toilet facility; 3 Sub-Centres had electricity supply; none of the Sub-Centres had provision for an inverter or solar energy source; 8 Sub-Centres had provision for drinking water; 3 Sub-Centres had provision of phone with the service providers; none of the Sub-Centres reported to have any provision of vehicles for its staff; 8 Sub-Centres had examination table; 9 Sub-Centres had writing tables; 4 Sub-Centres reported to have labour table provided at their health centres.

With regard to the availability of various services at the selected Sub-Centres (SCs), it was reported that out of 11 selected Sub-Centres together in Almora district and Haridwar district-9 Sub-Centres reported to have facility for early registration of the pregnant women. 9 Sub-Centres had the facility for measurement of weight and height; 9 Sub-Centres had facility of instrument for measurement of blood pressure; 9 Sub-Centres had facility for abdominal examination; 7 Sub-Centres had facility for breast examination; 9 Sub-Centres had facility for providing IFA tablets to the pregnant women; 9 Sub-Centres had facility for TT vaccination; 9 Sub-Centres had facility for anemia treatment; 7 Sub-Centres had facility for haemoglobin estimation; 4 Sub-Centres had facility for urine test for albumin and sugar; 8 Sub-Centres had facilities for identifying high risk pregnancy; 9 Sub-Centres had facility of counselling for diet and rest, just two Sub-Centres had facility for institutional delivery at their centres; 9 Sub-Centres had provisions of untied fund at the centres; only 3 Sub-Centres had provision for disbursement of cash incentive under Janani Suraksha Yojana (JSY); 9 Sub-Centres were engaging into monthly health day at Anganwadi Centres; 4 Sub-Centres had 24x7 services available at their centres.

- Primary Health Centre (PHC)

The Primary Health Centres (PHCs) are set up as a vital part of community development programme. Presently, the PHC covers a population of 20,000-30,000 (depending upon the geographical location) and occupies a place between a Sub-Centre at the most peripheral level and Community Health Centre at block level. The newly revised IPHS for PHC considers the services, infrastructure, manpower, equipment and medicines into two categories of essential (minimum assured services) and desirable (the ideal level services). From the point of view of infrastructure overall it falls short with 94

PHCs in Uttarakhand as per RHS data (2012) of MoHFW. The suggested layout of PHC includes the building space and other facilities, like manpower, equipment, furniture and medicines needed for providing the assured and desirable services at the PHC.

At the Primary Health Centre (PHC) level, overall a sample of three maternal health institutions in Almora district was surveyed in Uttarakhand. These three primary health centres all, in the hill district (Almora) included PHC Bharkinda Salt, PHC Additional Daulaghat, and PHC Hawalbagh.

With regard to availability of human resources at the primary health centre level, it was reported that 2 primary health centres had Male Medical officers, while none of the primary health centres reported to have a female Medical Officer at their centres; all the 3 primary health centres had pharmacist available there, which included one male AYUSH pharmacist, one female multi-purpose worker (MPW), and one primary health centre had a staff nurse; none of the primary health centre had either a lab technician or a AYUSH practitioner; while only one primary health worker had a female health worker available at its centre.

With regards to availability of infrastructure at the Primary Health Centre (PHC) level it was reported that out of a total of 3 selected sample of PHCs– 2 of the Primary Health Centres had the facility of waiting room; all the 3 primary health centres had facility of OPD room; all the 3 Primary Health Centres had facility of IPD wards; 2 primary health centres had IPD Bed occupancy in their centres' one primary health centre had facility of Labour room; all the 3 Primary Health Centres had facility of OT and minor dressing room; only one Primary Health Centre had facility of laboratory; and none of the Primary Health Centres had facility of general store in their centres; only one primary health centre had provision of separate counselling area; only one Primary Health Centre had a provision of a separate office room; all the 3 primary health centres had sufficient staff residence for accommodation; 2 Primary Health Centres had provision of electricity; one Primary Health Centres had inverter for alternate solar energy system; one Primary Health Centre had provision of safe drinking water; none of the Primary Health Centres reported about the provision of telephone as well as facility of ambulance with them.

With regard to the availability of various services at the selected Primary Health Centres (PHC) level it was reported that out of 3 selected Primary Health Centres in hills (Almora district)– 2 of the Primary Health Centres had facility of early registration of pregnant women; all the 3 Primary Health Centres had facility of measurement of weight and height; all the 3 Primary Health Centres had facility of measurement of blood pressure; 2 Primary Health Centres had facilities for each abdominal examination, breast examination, supplementation of IFA tablets, TT vaccinations, anaemic treatment, haemoglobin estimation, urine test for albumin and sugar, identification of high risk pregnancy, counselling on diet and rest, institutional normal delivery facility, disbursement of cash investment under JSY, and just one Primary Health Centre had facility for 24×7 services at their centres.

However, it was felt that the quality of care at the medical institutions particularly at Primary Health Centres and sub-centres needs to be improved to provide services for normal deliveries.

- Community Health Centre (CHC)

The Community Health Centres (CHCs) comprise the secondary level of health care, intended to provide referral as well as specialist health care to the rural population. Unlike Sub-Centre and PHCs, the CHCs are of one type only and operate as Block level health administrative unit and also porter for referrals to higher level of facilities. The IPHS (CHC) takes into account the services, infrastructure, manpower, equipment and medicines in two categories of essential (minimum assured services) and desirable (the ideal level services). All essential services in the CHC are required to be made available, which includes routine and emergency care in Surgery, Medicine, Obstetrics and Gynaecology, Paediatrics, together with all the National Health Programmes. With regard to rural health, the objective is to establish one Community Health Centre (CHC) for a population of one lakh. However, as per RHS data (2012) of MoHFW from the point of view of infrastructure and facilities overall it falls short with 28 CHCs in Uttarakhand.

At the level of Community Health Centre (CHC), overall a sample of seven maternal health institutions (3 in Almora district and 4 in

Haridwar district) were surveyed in Uttarakhand. The three Community Health Centres in Hill district (Almora) included CHC Dwalaghat, CHC Bhikya Saitha Salt and CHC Base Hospital; and the other four selected Community Health Centres in plain district (Haridwar) included CHC Bahadarabad, CHC Jawalapur, CHC Khanpur and CHC Laksar.

With regard to the availability of human resources at the Community Health Centre level, it was reported that 4 Community Health Centres had physicians; 4 Community Health Centres had general surgeons; 3 Community Health Centres had Pediatricians; 3 community health centres had obstrecticians and Gynecologists; one Community Health Centre had an Anaesthetist; 5 Community Health Centres had general duty medical officers; 2 Community Health Centres had AYUSH specialist; 4 Community Health Centres had AYUSH General Duty Medical Officers; 5 Community Health Centres had staff nurse there; 4 Community Health Centres had ANMs; 2 Community Health Centres had Radiographers; and 4 Community health centres reported to have Laboratory Technicians at their centres.

With regard to the availability of infrastructures at the level of Community Health Centres, it was reported that 6 of the Community Health Centres had labour room at their centres; 6 Community Health Centres had operation theatres; 6 Community Health Centres had IPD ward; 4 Community Health Centres had x-ray rooms; 4 Community Health Centres had laboratory; 4 Community Health Centres had separate counselling area; 5 Community Health Centres had full time electricity; 6 Community Health Centres had provisions of inverter for the purpose of solar energy; 5 Community Health Centres had provision for safe drinking water; 4 Community Health Centres had telephone facility; 5 Community Health Centres had facility for Ambulance; none of the Community Health Centres reported to have any vehicle facility for its staff.

With regards to the availability of various services at the selected Community Health Centres, it was reported that out of seven selected CHCs together in Almora district and Haridwar district– 6 of the Community Health Centres reported to have facility for early registration of the pregnant women; 6 Community Health Centres had facility for measurement of weight and height; 6 Community

Health Centres had facility for measurement of blood pressure; 5 Community Health Centres had facility for abdominal examination; 4 Community Health Centres had facility for breast examination; 6 Community Health Centres had provision for IFA supplementation; 6 Community Health Centres had provision for TT vaccination; 6 Community Health Centres had provisions for treatment of anaemia; 5 Community Health Centres had facility for haemoglobin estimation; 5 Community Health Centres had facility for urine test for albumin and sugar; only one of the selected Community Health Centres had ultrasound facility; 4 Community Health Centres had facility for blood group identification; only 2 of the selected Community Health Centres had facility for identification of high risk pregnancy; 4 Community Health Centres had blood storage facility; only 3 Community Health Centres were upgraded as FRU; 5 Community Health Centres had facility for counselling on diet and rest; 5 Community Health Centres had facilities for institutional normal delivery'; 2 Community Health Centres had facility for c-section and high risk delivery care; 5 Community Health Centres had 24×7 services at their end' and 5 Community Health Centres reported to have disbursement of cash incentive under Janani Suraksha Yojana (JSY).

- District Hospital (DH)

District Hospital is a hospital at the secondary referral level that is responsible for a district of a defined geographical area comprising of a defined population. Its purpose is to provide all-inclusive secondary health care services to the people in the district at a satisfactory level of quality and being sensitive to the requirements of people and referring centres. Every district is expected to have a district hospital having provisions for quality assurance in clinics, laboratories, blood bank, ward unit, pharmacies, and emergency services.

At the district level, a total of two hospitals one each in hills (Almora district) and one in plains (Haridwar district) were surveyed for the purpose of the study. These two district hospitals included one district hospital in Almora district and one in Haridwar district. District hospital in Almora reported to have 50 institutional deliveries on an average monthly basis, while Mahila Chikitsalaya Haridwar reported to have 200 institutional deliveries on an average monthly basis. With regards to the availability of human resources at the District Hospital level, it was reported that only one of these two hospitals under survey had physician, general surgeon, paediatrician, obstetrician and gynaecologist, anaesthetist, male General Duty Medical Officer, Female General Duty Medical Officer, AYUSH specialist, staff nurse and laboratory technician; while none had AYUSH General Duty medical officer, ANM, and radiographer.

With regard to availability of infrastructure at the district hospital level, it was reported that both of them had labour room, operation theatres, IPD ward, X-ray room, laboratory, electricity supply, safe drinking water, telephone, ambulance, and vehicle for staff.

With regard to availability of maternal health services, both the district hospitals in Almora district and in Hardwar district reported that they have the maternal health services like - early registration of pregnant women; measurement of weight and height, measurement of blood pressure, abdominal examination; breast examination; supplementation of IFA tablets; TT vaccination; estimation of haemoglobin; treatment of anaemia; urine test for albumin and sugar; identification of high risk pregnancies, counselling on diet and rest; institutional normal delivery. Facility for C-section and high risk delivery care; 24×7 services; and disbursement of cash incentive under Janani Suraksha Yojana (JSY).

Thus, ASHAs' knowledge on different aspects of maternal and child health aspects was reasonably well; however, a need is felt for strengthening knowledge about postnatal care particularly of the newborn, and identifying and dealing with complications during pregnancy and childbirth.

This chapter brings out the findings on service providers' awareness and utilization of the services among the target beneficiaries, through the questionnaires administered to the service providers in the selected areas to elicit relevant information. This chapter brings out the findings about their role and experiences in the JSY scheme vis-à-vis support provided by them to the mothers in their respective areas of operation.

Chapter - 6

Maternal Health Care and the Way Forward

As it is mentioned in the earlier chapters, the reason for taking up this study was to assess and analyse the high level of maternal mortality rate, despite in Uttarakhand it has been under the patronage of the Empowered Action Group (EAG) specially set up by the Government of India to look into area specific aspects for the holistic development of the people. Though Janani Suraksha Yojna was introduced in Uttarakhand in 2005, according to the official information by the government, based on health surveys conducted in Uttrakhand, MMR was at 188 in 2011 which is well above the expected goal of 100, though it was slightly lower than the all India indicator in that year which was higher at 212. In order to understand the underlying reasons for the high level of MMR in the broader context of the functioning of JSY, this study was initiated, with particular focus on the special geographical setting of the state and thus come out with both policy and programmatic recommendations.

Though it is a comparative study of two districts, Haridwar, a district in the plains and Almora, in the hills, lessons drawn from the experiences of the respondents can be well utilized and expanded to understand the functioning of JSY in the state and take appropriate measures to improve the functioning.

This chapter contains two major sections, namely, major findings of the Study and recommendations based on the study.

6.1 Major Findings

In order to develop a scientific and nuanced understanding of the access and utilization of JSY by the mothers and how this programme had promoted institutional delivery with institutional, infrastructural and health personnel support, the respondents were classified into three categories and analyzed accordingly.

a. Those sample respondent mothers during the period of study who did not access JSY

b. Those sample respondent mothers who partly accessed JSY, either began with JSY and moved out or at some point of time accessed and utilized JSY

c. Those sample respondents who largely accessed and utilized JSY scheme

At the outset it is important to highlight that during the period of data collection from August 2013 to November 2013, no maternal death was reported in these two districts in the preceding one year, except one incident of still birth in Haridwar.

6.1.1 Non-access to JSY is still very high

The study reveals reasonably a good number of mothers who have kept themselves away completely from accessing and utilizing JSY. Out of the total number of respondents of the study 313, of which 210 were from Haridwar and 103 from Almora, about 23.3 per cent women respondent mothers, which is about 73 respondents either went in for private maternal care or followed traditional home based delivery. It is also important to note that out of the 73 respondents 70 are from Haridwar and only 3 are from Almora. Why only 33.3 per cent, which is one third of the sample respondents, out of 210 respondents of Haridwar preferred to be away from JSY raises many questions. An analysis of who did not access JSY reveals that the respondents feel that there is lack of good doctors and lack of basic facilities in government hospitals. On the contrary they are of the view that good services and care is provided by private maternal care centres. Some also said that fear of pregnancy complications led them to private hospitals. They felt that private hospitals are in a better position to handle complicated deliveries than government hospitals. From further analysis of these 73 respondents who did not access JSY, the following findings can be highlighted.

6.1.2 Drastic reduction in Home Delivery

While analyzing the access and utilization of 313 respondents in Haridwar and Almora it was strikingly clear that there has been drastic reduction in home deliveries. It was observed that only 5 respondent mothers (1.6 per cent), 2 from Haridwar and 3 from Almora had followed traditional home-based delivery. During focus group discussion it was revealed by the respondents that after the introduction of JSY, and the proactive awareness building programmes by the government, there is a strong realization among the women about the need to go for institutional delivery and avoid traditional home-based delivery even in remote villages in order to protect both the life of the mother and the child. This is a welcome development. Women also said that about a decade ago a number of women preferred home delivery for socio-cultural reasons. They felt that delivery as a 'private affair' feeling shy of talking about pregnancy related issues and problems. This traditional mindset has largely changed now and women, in general are talking about pregnancy related issues and preference to adopt institutional delivery.

It is also interesting to note that out of 5 respondents who adopted home delivery, only 2 are from Haridwar out of 210 respondents and 3 are from Almora out of 103 respondents. Among the 2 women from Haridwar, one woman was from OBC category and one was from general category. Among the three from Almora, 2 were from SC/ST category and one was from general category.

6.1.3 Attraction to Private maternal care in the plains seems to be high

It is to be noted that out of 313 respondents, 68 respondents opted for private maternal care and interestingly all the respondents are from Haridwar and no one out of 103 respondents in Almora went to private maternal care. Respondents in Almora have completely kept themselves away from private maternal care. A further analysis of the 68 respondents who opted for private maternal care revealed the phenomenon that out of these, 66.7 per cent belong to general caste category, 35.4 per cent belong to OBC and only 20.5 per cent belong to SC/ST category. While it is difficult to state why a good many mothers preferred private maternal care in Haridwar and none in Almora, one conclusion can be drawn. There are more number of private maternal hospitals in Haridwar, the plain district and Almora being a hilly terrain there are not many private maternal care hospitals. While talking to mothers they said that the private maternal care centres take special efforts to attract or woo the pregnant mothers, at times even there is threat about pregnancy complications. Some mothers who get scared of such information prefer to go to private maternal care centres than accessing JSY scheme. The analysis of the perception of the service provided substantiated this conclusion that 22 out of 33 service providers, mainly the ASHAs stated that in Haridwar pregnant mothers prefer private institutions than the government health care institution.

6.1.4 Some took initial interest in JSY but did not sustain

It is also important to note that about 67 respondents which are about 21.4 per cent, a little less than who completely kept themselves away from JSY as mentioned above (73 respondents) showed initial interest in JSY but slowly moved away from JSY and ended up either in private or home delivery. Among 67, about 49 are from Haridwar and 18 are from Almora. In Almora of the 18 respondents 15 of them after showing initial interest in JSY later ended up in home delivery. Of those 15 who had delivered in home, 9 belong to SC/ST category and 6 belonged to general category. This phenomenon was further underlined by Asha workers of Almora that a number of pregnant mothers still prefer to have home delivery due to cultural reasons and taboos attached to child birth. This seems to be strong among some sections of dalits and tribals.

In Haridwar out of 49 respondents who moved away from JSY after initial enthusiasm, almost equal number of respondents about 24 ended up in home delivery and about 22 ended up in private maternity care centres. Out of these 46, 28 belong to SC/ST category and 15 belong to OBC. It shows that a reasonable number of SC/ST and OBC pregnant women showed initial interest in JSY but for various reasons did not sustain and ended up either in home delivery or in private maternity care.

6.1.5 Access and Utilization of JSY is very high in Almora than Haridwar

Analysis of access and utilization of JSY to a large extent revealed that out of 313 respondents only 173 women which is about 55.3 per cent accessed and utilized JSY to a large extent. This means that these accessed and utilized prenatal care, delivery and post natal care through JSY. It is surprising to note that despite various efforts made by the government, including area specific programmes developed by EAG only just above 50 per cent has largely utilized JSY. This is a matter of great concern.

A further analysis shows that out of 173 who benefited by JSY, 91 are from Haridwar and 82 are from Almora. With the total sample respondents from Almora being 103, it is good to note that 82 respondents, 79.6 per cent accessed and utilized JSY largely. Whereas, in Haridwar the percentage of women who accessed JSY largely is only 43.3 per cent which is much below the half way mark.

6.1.6 SC/ST have largely accessed and utilized JSY

In terms of social categories, out of 173, SC/ST beneficiaries stand at 108 (62.4 per cent), OBC are 31 (17.9 per cent) and those who belong to general category are 34 (19.7 per cent). In other words it can be concluded that SC/ST women are the ones who have largely accessed and utilized JSY in the two districts.

The utilization of JSY in Almora is very high among SC/STs. Out of 60 respondents belonging SC/ST category in Almora 48 (80 per cent) have largely accessed and utilized JSY where as in Haridwar proportionately it is only 53.6 per cent of women belonging to SC/ST have largely accessed JSY. This is supplemented by the views of service providers that generally women of Scheduled Castes approach the sub-centres to avail ante-natal and post-natal care.

6.1.7 ANC was effectively utilized than Delivery and PNC care

Access and utilization of ANC, delivery and PNC was analyzed using four major variables, namely, availability, accessibility, affordability and acceptability. Among the 173 who largely accessed and utilized JSY, about 88.9 per cent felt that they effectively utilized ANC. When questions were asked about utilization of delivery and PNC only about 54.2 per cent and 52.4 per cent respectively said that they utilized delivery and PNC without much difficulty. In other words, even among those who have largely benefitted by JSY when it comes to delivery and PNC there is distancing from the scheme.

6.1.8 Problems faced in Institutional Delivery and PNC

Access and utilization of institutional delivery service was analysed through availability, accessibility and affordability. Among the 173 beneficiary respondents largely benefitting from Janani Suraksha Yojana, 10.2 per cent experienced difficulty in terms of availing, accessing and affording the services. Difficulties are experienced in terms of availing services due to geographical distance of institutions. It was evident that respondents of Almora experience distance as a major difficulty than those respondents in Haridwar. This trend was also seen in the post natal care stage. In other words, despite geographical distance pregnant mothers travel and access ANC care but find it difficult to access delivery care and PNC care. The respondents also said that ASHA workers are not able to arrange conveyance in some cases for delivery and post natal care. This conclusion was confirmed by the views of ASHA workers. The ASHA workers admitted that at times they find it difficult to get transport facility, especially in the hilly terrains.

6.1.9 Concerns for Institutional support for ASHA

It was found that health Service providers do not have arrangements for night stay in most institutions. In many instances ASHA workers who accompany the pregnant women to the health facility for institutional delivery are often made to stay in the morgue during the night. Some ASHA workers feel demotivated by this arrangement.

6.1.10 Service providers not trained in safe delivery in normal circumstances

Most service providers including ASHA and ANM in both Haridwar and Almora were trained to undertake the various activities under ante-natal care as well as the post-natal care for the pregnant women. But only 20 per cent of them in Almora and 27 per cent in Haridwar were formally trained to carry out safe delivery in normal conditions. ASHA workers expressed that if they are trained well in safe delivery in normal circumstances they could carry out delivery, especially when there are difficulties in bringing mother to institutions for delivery. This is very much required in hilly district like Almora

6.1.11 JSY access in relation to educational and income status

Clearly, it appears that the lesser the educational level, the greater the likelihood of JSY use. In the same manner, lesser the income level, the greater the likelihood of JSY use. In summary there seems to be an inverse relationship with regard to access to JSY services. Higher the education status of mothers access is lower. High the income status of mothers access to JSY seems lower. These trends raise a fundamental question with regard to the objective of JSY. If the goal of JSY is to reduce MMR, it is important that all potential mothers access JSY, transcending education and income status. At present the image of JSY being largely meant only for the poor will reduce quality of health care. This has been the experience of various schemes of the government in the past. Moreover, it is also noticeable that mushrooming of private maternity hospitals has had considerable negative impact on JSY scheme and the way government medical institutions function. So any effort to improve JSY functioning has to be looked into in the broader context of emerging challenges from privatisation of health care systems in India.

6.1.12 Affordability reduces access to JSY in delivery and post-natal care in the Hills

Postnatal care is important for beneficiary mothers from the point of view of her health particularly soon after the delivery. In order to ensure easy affordability towards this end and meet the benefits of the counselling and services under this it is important to increase the incentive of the Auxiliary Nurse Midwife towards meeting the transportation costs incurred in the hilly terrain for the purpose of visiting the mothers at their homes, and thereby understanding the importance of institutional delivery and postnatal care.

6.1.13 Awareness about Janani Suraksha Yojana

Nearly one-third of the respondents out of total 313 including majority from the rural areas, especially in Haridwar district were somewhat aware about JSY, while the remaining were not informed about JSY and its component benefits and purpose. Many respondents were well aware of the usefulness of TT vaccination. Many were also aware of the importance of staying minimum for 48 hours in hospital. It is a matter of concern that regarding the importance of institutional delivery the awareness level was low among the respondents.

6.2 Recommendations

From the findings of the study the following recommendations are made which could be useful in other districts of Uttarakhand as well as in other states where JSY is implemented.

6.2.1 Evidences show that there is considerable reduction in MMR over the years and increase in utilization of JSY in Almorah and Haridwar. During 9 months of data collection it is found that non-access to JSY is still very high in the sample districts. Three factors clearly emerge for lack of access to JSY scheme among the sample respondents. Higher income families and educated ones seem to prefer private health care. Moreover, increase in private hospitals also has impact in lack of access to JSY, especially in Haridwar. From physical verification it is evidently clear that a number of private maternity health care centres have come up in the plains than the hills which continue to woo the mothers with various strategies. Some women are becoming victims to the false propaganda that private is better and efficient than government run hospitals. If the women have the means they prefer private maternity care to JSY scheme.

6.2.2 It is also found that traditional home-based delivery is still practiced in some pockets especially among the poor and vulnerable communities. If MMR has to be reduced to a desired level keeping in mind the emerging paradigm of health as human right it is important that state must take all efforts to ensure that there is 100 per cent institutional delivery. The state has to draw up a plan to identify those mothers and areas and find out the reasons for continuing to practise home-based delivery. Necessary motivational and educational programmes need to be organised so that progressively there will be zero percentage of home-based deliveries. To this extent the ASHA workers could be empowered and even rewarded in identifying home-based deliveries and convert them into institutional deliveries.

6.2.3 Study also brings out the fact that large number of mothers have registered with JSY but the number reduces progressively as they access pre-natal, delivery, and post natal care. In other words initial enthusiasm to access JSY vanishes slowly and mothers for various reasons switch over to private maternity care. Moreover, it was also found that number of mothers who access ANC reduces when it comes to delivery and much less in post-natal care. This trend calls for deeper study into the phenomenon and state has to take remedial measure to that those who register under JSY undergo all three stages and end up in quality institutional delivery and reduction in IMR. State also has to look into private medical practitioners that they do not exploit the vulnerability of pregnant women through false propaganda and some control mechanism and monitoring systems are to be established.

6.2.4 The reason for Almora respondents facing problems in post-natal care is one related to distance. The respondents find it difficult to travel far along with their new born babies. So they do access post natal care provided in JSY. It is important that a functional and a safe facility at Sub-Centre nearer to home with a referral connection is the need particularly in hilly terrains. The principle should be that every locale should have a 24×7 functional Sub-Centre or a PHC with at least skilled birth attendant, basic emergency obstetric and newborn care within half-hour access time. In special circumstance transportation facilities could be arranged by the maternity centres to bring the mother and child for post-natal care.

6.2.5 In Haridwar it was found that within the caste categories, from general category nearly 67 per cent prefer private maternity care and 35.4 per cent from OBCs. Though this phenomenon is not unusual, given that generally OBCs and general category women are likely to be better off in education and income, it requires further probing to find out the blocks experienced by General and OBC community women in accessing JSY. JSY as a scheme cannot be equated to any social categories. It has to promote institutional and safe delivery of all women transcending social and economic indicators with the ultimate purpose of reducing MMR and increasing safe delivery.

6.2.6 There is a need for periodic trainings of ASHAs and ANMs to provide them hands on skills and techniques besides appreciation of their work. Although, ASHA unlike traditional *dai*, or anganwadi worker or ANM is designated to make frequent post-natal and newborn visits, she needs to be trained with adequate skills to convert these into early detection of any sickness or even into promotion of positive health practices.

6.2.7 While the ASHAs and ANMs seem to possess good knowledge on JSY, their communication skills needs to be strengthened so that they could effectively speak to the potential women the importance and benefits of JSY as well as institutional and safe delivery.

6.2.8 Care should be taken to maintain that cash incentive be paid on the day of delivery. If not then on the second day. Further delays beyond this will be intolerable and less inviting. Delay in payment or asking women to visit again to receive incentives will go against entitlement as a right. If discharge is likely to happen late in the evening or night and the accounts/cash section might be closed by then, the imbursement should be made earlier, instead of asking the woman to come later. If the woman is in bed with a newborn baby, no further identity proof is required and payment must be done without any delay. Still, if for whatever reason this cannot be made, then the responsibility of reaching the money to her house must be the norm and not asking the women to visit again to receive the incentive.

6.2.9 No doubt the best practice to be followed in all circumstances is payment by account payee cheque. Cash payment could lead to many other complications and at times to bribery and forced commission. However, considering the specific geographical nature of Almora, a hilly terrain district, an alternative mode of JSY payments could be thought of. The present account payee cheques system seems to be causing undue delay for the beneficiaries in getting the benefits. In some cases as the mothers do not have a bank account the cheque payment itself is causing difficulties particularly in hilly terrain. This phenomenon gets complicated wherever there is less availability of transport. One way to address this difficulty, though not to fool proof system, to issue bearer cheque in the place of account payee cheque.

6.2.10 Respondents have stated that at times there is non-cooperation of ANMs and ASHAs. On the other hand ANM/ASHA had complained of over workload and stated that they are asked to do all sorts of works which in normal circumstances professionally trained people are expected to carry out. Over burdening of ASHA workers only will weaken their services. Adequate steps are to be taken for the smooth functioning of ANMs and ASHAs. This will enable the health care providers to deliver health care services in a friendly manner without stress.

6.2.11 There is a need to provide proper facilities for ASHA workers for night stay in the health institution wherever she accompanies women for institutional delivery. It has been reported that ASHA workers are often forced to sleep in unhygienic places which is a de-motivating factor. Every delivery centre must be equipped with proper place for rest for ASHA workers since they are expected to serve women on 24 x 7.

6.2.12 The state seems to have done good propaganda about JSY to spread general awareness among women. However, now it is time to look at the gaps as mentioned above and adopt suitable awareness strategies to reduce the existing gaps and make JSY a successful scheme.

This study has brought out clearly the benefits of JSY among the sample respondents in two geographically distinct districts - Almora and Haridwar in Uttarakhand. While the study has identified a number of contributing factors for the success of JSY in drastically reducing MMR it has also identified gaps in the implementation of the scheme. It is crucial that JSY is seen as a scheme to promote institutional and safe delivery than a scheme for the poor. In a profit oriented economy health concerns have become tradable. The private players seem to be making efforts to woo the pregnant women to their side to expand their business. The need of the hour is to develop health as human rights issue and not just a matter of welfare measure promoted by the state. Every woman has to demand the state to provide quality maternity care as a matter of right than charity. Lessons could be drawn from this study carried out in two sample districts and could be used in other districts of Uttarakhand and elsewhere in the county. What is emerging from the study is that from a general approach of promoting institutional and safe delivery, which was the need of the hours a decade ago, gaps in the implementation are to be paid attention to. Focused action is indispensable towards meeting goals for reduction of maternal mortality and safe motherhood.

Bibliography

- Bannerji, D. (1985). Health and Family Planning Services in India: An Epidemiological Socio-cultural and Political Analysis and a Perspective, Lok Prakash, New Delhi.
- Baqui A.H., Williams E.K., Darmstadt G.L., Kumar V., Kiran T.U. , Panwar D. (2007). Newborn care in Rural Uttar Pradesh. Indian J Pediatr 2007; 74(3) :241-247.
- Bir Thaneshwar (2006). Health Sector Reform in India: Perspectives and Issues, Arise Publishers and Distributors, Delhi.
- Census, (2001). Registrar General of India, Government of India, New Delhi.
- Census (2011). Registrar General of India, Government of India, New Delhi.
- CRR (2008). Maternal Mortality in India, Using international and constitutional law to promote accountability and change, Centre for Reproductive Rights, New York.
- Chauhan Alok and K.V. Yadav (2012). "Determinants of Institutional and Safe Delivery in Hanumangarh District (Rajasthan): A Multivariate Analysis", Indian Journal of Maternal and Child Health, Vol. 14(1) Jan-March.
- Constella Futures (2012). Community–based Workers Improve Health Outcomes in Uttarakhand, Gurgaon, India, Constella Futures.
- CES (2009). Coverage Evaluation Survey, India. UNICEF India Office, Delhi.
- Dasgupta, Urmila, Subhrajyoti Naskar, Anima Haldar and Sarmila Malik (2012). "Antenatal care service utilization and social correlates of beneficiaries: an experience from a teaching hospital of a metropolitan city", Indian Journal of Maternal and Child Health, Vol. 14(2) April-June.
- Deshpande, R.V. (2011). "Is Janani Suraksha Yojana (JSY) contributing to the reduction of maternal and infant mortality? An insight from Karnataka". The Journal of Family Welfare, Vol. 57, No. 1, June-2011.
- DRS (2009). Concurrent Assessment of Janani Surakhsa Yojana (JSY) Scheme in Selected State of India, 2008, Bihar, Madhya Pradesh, Orissa, Rajasthan, Uttar Pradesh, Development and Research Services (P) Ltd, New Delhi.

- Gaur Neeraj, Dhiraj Srivastava, Paharam Adhikari and Anumita Shahi (2012). "A Desk Review to Assess the Impact of Janani Suraksha Yojana on Various MCH Indicators in District Gwalior", International Journal of Collaborative Research on Internal Medicine and Public Health, Vol. 4, No. 8.
- Government of Rajasthan (2007). Executive Summary: The Rajasthan Health System Development Project (RHSDP). Government of Rajasthan, Jaipur.
- Gupta Sanjeev K, Dinesh K. Pal, Rajesh Tiwari, Rajesh Garg, Ashish K. Shrivastava, Radha Sarawagi, Rajkumar Patil, Lokesh Agarwal, Prashant Gupta, Chandrakant Lahariya (2012). "Impact of Janani Suraksha Yojana on Institutional Delivery Rate and Maternal Morbidity and Mortality: An Observational Study in India", Journal of Health, Population and Nutrition, Vol. 30, No. 4, December.
- Gupta, S.K, D.K. Pal, R.Tiwari, R. Garg, R. Sarasagi, A.K. Shrivastava, (2010), "Antenatal Characteristics of the Beneficiaries of Janani Suraksha Yojana in a tertiary Care Hospital in Madhya Pradesh", Indian Journal of Maternal and Child Health, Vol. 12(2) April-June.
- Haralkar S.J, P.D. Pore, S.V. Khandekar, A.S. Haralkar and Tapare, (2012). "Study of Maternal Mortality at Tertiary Govt. Hospital in Solapur, Western Maharashtra", Indian Journal of Maternal and Child Health, Vol. 14(2) April-June.
- IIPS and Macro International. (2007). *National Family Health Survey (NFHS-3), 2005–06: India, Volume 1*. Mumbai.
- Kaulagekar-Nagarkar Arti, Manali Pandit and Dhanashree Ramdas, (2012). "Place of delivery and factors influencing the choice among urban slum women from Pimpri-Chinchwad municipal area, Maharashtra", Indian Journal of Maternal and Child Health, Vol. 14 (1) Jan-March.
- Khan M.E, Avishek Hazra and Isha Bhatnagar, (2010). "Impact of Janani Suraksha Yojana on Selected Family Health Behaviors in Rural Uttar Pradesh", The Journal of Family Welfare, Vol. 56, Special Issue.
- Khanna Renu and Subha Sri B, (2012). "Maternal Health Policy in India-From Institutional Deliveries to Safe Deliveries", SAHAJ, August.
- KLP (2009). UNICEF highlights maternal mortality in India. Karnataka Learning Partnership, January 25.
- Kumar Satish (2010). "Reducing Maternal Mortality in India: Policy, Equity and Quality Issues", Indian Journal of Public Health, Vol. 54, Issue 2, April-June.
- Kundu Soma (2010). "Differentials in Health Care Access in India: The Case of MCH Services, Indian Journal of Gender Studies", Vol. 17, No. 1, January-April.

- Lahariya Chandrakant (2009). "Cash Incentive for Institutional Delivery: Linking with Antenatal and Postnatal Care May Ensure 'Continuum of Care' in India", Indian Journal of Community Medicine, Vol. 34(1), January.
- Lim, S.S., L. Dandona, J.A. Hoisington et al. (2010). "India's *Janani Suraksha Yojana*, a conditional cash transfer programme to increase births in health facilities: An impact evaluation," *The Lancet,* 375(9730):1939–2050.
- Mavlankar D.V, Kranti S. Vora, K.V. Ramani, Parvathy Raman, Bharti Sharma, and Mudita Upadhyaya, 2009."Maternal Health in Gujarat, Inda: A Case Study", Journal of Health, Population and Nutrition, Vol. 27, No. 2, April.
- MOHFW, (2005). Ministry of Health and Family Welfare, *National Rural Health Mission (2005–2012)*. Mission Document. Government of India, New Delhi.
- MOHFW, (2006). Ministry of Health and Family Welfare, *Janani Suraksha Yojana: Features and Frequently Asked Questions and Answers*. Government of India, New Delhi: http://mohfw.nic.in/dofwwebsite/JSY_features_FAQ_Nov_2006.htm.
- MoHFW, (2009). Concurrent Evaluation of National Rural Health Mission, IIPS, Mumbai.
- My-Heart, (2010). Maternal Mortality in Orissa: An Epidemiological Study, Bhubhneshwar, India.
- Nandan Deoki and Dinesh Agarwal, (2012). "Human Resource for Health in India: Urgent Need for Reform, Indian Journal of Community Medicine", Vol. 37 Issue 4, October.
- Nayar, K.R, (2007), Social Exclusion, "Caste and Health: A review based on the social determinants framework", Indian Journal of Medical Research, 126, October.
- Nayar, K.R, (2011). "India's country experience in addressing social exclusion in maternal and child health", presented in World Conference on Social Determinants of Health, held 19-21 October 2011, in Rio de Janeiro, Brazil.
- NFHS-III, 2004-05. National Family Health Survey-3 (NFHS-3), IIPS, Mumbai.
- NHSRC, (2011). Program Evaluation of Janani Suraksha Yojana, MoHFWS, New Delhi.
- SRS, (2011). *Sample Registration System (2007-2009 Special bulletin on maternal mortality in India 2007–09,* New Delhi: Office of the Registrar General, India.
- Planning Commission, (2011), Evaluation Study of National Rural Health Mission (NRHM) in 7 States, Programme Evaluation Organisation, (GoI), New Delhi.

- Rajaretnam, T, R.V. Deshpande, V.B. Joshi, and Purujit Praharaj, (2005). "Problems Faced by the Field Level Service Providers in Delivering the Basic Maternal and Child Health Services: A Qualitative Study in Bellary and Raichur Districts of Karanataka State", IIPS, Mumbai.
- Rao Krishna D. et al. (2010), "Health Worker attitudes Toward Rural Service in India, Result from Qualitative Research", Health, Nutrition and Population unit of World Bank November.
- Rao Mohan, (1998). "India's Augean Stables: The Unfinished Health Agenda", in Women's Health, Public Policy and Community Action (ed), Institute of Social Studies Trust.
- Rogen, Shanna Elaine B. and Ma. Virginia R. Olveña, (2004). "Factors Affecting Maternal Health Utilization in the Philippines", 9th National convention on Statistics, National Statistics Office, Manila.
- Rural Health Statistics (RHS), (2011). Statistics Division of Ministry of Health and Family Welfare, GoI, New Delhi.
- Sahu Divya, N.K, Gandhi and G.P. Soni, (2012). "Knowledge and Utilization of Janani Suraksha Yojana (JSY): An Epidemiological Study", Indian Journal of Maternal and Child Health, Vol. 14 (1) Jan-March.
- Shariff Abusaleh and Geeta Singh, (2002). "Determinants of Maternal Health Care Utlisation in India: Evidence from a Recent Household Survey", Working paper series No. 85, National Council for Applied Economics Research, New Delhi.
- Sharma, Ramakant, (2008). "Janani Suraksha Yojana: A Study of the Implementation Status in Selected Districts of Rajasthan, Population Research Centre", Mohanlal Sukhadia University, Udaipur.
- Singh Manish K, JV Singh, N. Ahmad, Reema Kumari and A. Khanna, (2010). "Factors Influencing Utilization of ASHA Services Under NRHM in Relation to Maternal Health in Rural Lucknow", Indian Journal of Community Medicine, vol. 35 Issue 3, July.
- Singh S K, Awadhesh Kumar Singh, (2006). Reproductive Child Health in the North East Region, Serials Publication, New Delhi.
- Singh Susheela, Lisa Remez, Usha Ram, Ann M. Moore and Suzette Audam, (2009). Barriers to Safe Motherhood in India, New York: Guttmacher Institute.
- Singh, Abha Lakshmi (ed) and Ifran Sabir and Sarfraj Asghar, (2005). Rural Women: Work and Health, The Women Press, Delhi.
- Soman, Krishna, (1998). Planning for Women's Health: The Indian Experience in Women's Health, Public Policy and Community Action (ed), Manohar Publishers and Distributors, New Delhi
- Srinivasan, K. C.P Prakasham, T. Rajaretnam and P. Praharaj, (2006). Expanding Basic Maternal and Child Health Services: An Operations Research Project with Birth-based Approach, IIPS, Mumbai.

- UNICEF, (2009). Coverage Evaluation Survey, India. UNICEF, New Delhi.
- UNFPA (2009). *Concurrent Assessment of Janani Suraksha Yojana (JSY) Scheme in Selected States of India, 2008*. World Health Organization 2005. World Health Report, Geneva: WHO.
- World Vision and the Nossal Institute for Global Health, (2008). Strategies that work, Melbourne, Australia.
- Yusuf Muhammad and Hem Borker, (2009). Privatization of Reproductive and Child Health Services: Implications on Muslim Women, in "Health Matters: India's Health Services", Who Benefits?" Edited by Sinha Archana, John TA, Indian Social Institute, Delhi.

Index